The

Eliminate Self-Sabotage

In 30 Minutes or Less

For Success, Wealth, Love and Happiness!

By Michael Craig

Foreword by Dr. Brenda Wade

Publisher Data & Legal Information

Logical Soul LLC
6050 Peachtree Parkway, Ste 240-340L
Norcross, Georgia 30092 USA
publisher@logicalsoul.com

Copyright © 2010-2016 by Michael Craig.
All rights reserved. No part of this book may be reproduced, stored in a retrieval system or transmitted in any form or by any means electronic, mechanical, photocopying, recording, or otherwise without express written permission of the author. "Logical Soul" is the Registered Trademark of Michael Craig and Logical Soul LLC.

Library of Congress Cataloging-in-Publication Data
Craig, Michael
    The Logical Soul: Eliminate Self-Sabotage in 30 Minutes or Less for Success, Wealth, Love & Happiness, 4th Ed.
    Includes Index
    1. Inner Child   2. Self-Help
       ISBN-13: 978-0-9800674-4-6
       LCCN: 2010901610 (2010 Edition)

Editor: Vandana Chadha
Cover design: Audrey Jones and Gaurav Sikka.
Layout & Index: Michael Craig and Vandana Chadha.

Artwork and general photography by author, Brigitte Craig, Carol Reister, www.istockphotos.com, Ed Steeley, and family archives. Every attempt has been made by the author to acknowledge the sources used for the material in this book. If there has been any omission, contact the author or publisher.

Disclaimer: No responsibility or liability is assumed by the author or publisher for any injury, damage and/or loss sustained to persons or property as a result of using the methods, instructions or ideas contained in the material herein, and/or for any negligence arising from same use. The views and opinions expressed in this book are strictly those of the author who is neither a medical doctor nor a psychologist. Readers are advised to seek professional advice before using or practicing any of the material or techniques contained herein.

ABOUT THE AUTHOR

MICHAEL CRAIG was born in Savannah, Georgia, USA, to an architect father and artist mother. Despite a relatively happy childhood, Michael's later years were marred by failure and self-sabotage. He was twice-divorced, bankrupt, went from job to job, and pushed away opportunities as he sought to hide from life experiences. A series of inner awakening experiences before his mid-twenties – and the inevitable crashes that followed – prompted Michael to coin the phrase "Post-Guru Syndrome" to describe this period of destructive nihilism.

After graduating **Life Chiropractic College** in 1983, Dr. Craig set up a practice in Atlanta. Years of financial struggles eventually netted him enough money to embark on a journey to Asia. There he spent four months in Kalibuwila Hospital in **Sri Lanka** studying forms of alternative medicine: acupuncture, homeopathy, laser therapy, and minor surgery.

It was Dr. Craig's experiences in Sri Lanka, and his subsequent study of Hawaiian Huna practices, that opened his eyes to new ways of natural healing by *intent*, and the true meaning of Socrates' injunction to "Know Thyself." He spent the next twenty years pursuing a total curative method that incorporated both ancient and modern techniques. The **Logical Soul®** is the result of this search.

Dr. Craig currently lives with his wife of 21+ years in the Atlanta area. He gives lectures, sees private clients, and promotes both his own and affiliate products online. He may be reached via website (www.logicalsoul.com), email (drcraig@logicalsoul.com), or by calling **(404) 348-4672.**

This book is dedicated to my beloved **Soma** (Brigitte), whose encouragement and constant devotion made this work possible.

TESTIMONIALS

"Michael you've definitely hit the nail on the head with The Logical Soul®! The techniques you recommend are pure genius, and I'm already envisioning the many lives that will be positively impacted by your insights! GREAT job for sure!"
- **Jason Oman**
#1 Best-Selling Author,
Conversations with Millionaires.
www.JasonOman.com

"It's totally law of attraction, it's totally responsibility; it's totally taking charge of your life. I love it . . . We're in perfect resonance! I'm yours; you got me at 'hello'!"
- **Raymond Aaron**
Author, *Double Your Income Doing What You Love*
www.MonthlyMentor.com

"In my years of hanging around successful people long enough to become one myself, I'm convinced that you absolutely need both an INTENSE DESIRE and EXTREME FOCUS in order to achieve the success you deserve and desire. This book helps unlock these secrets and is a definite MUST READ!"
- **Devon Brown**
www.RenegadeSuccess.com

"I had anxiety bad . . . to the point it made me sick. It was a mental problem that got so bad it became a physical problem. I never knew how to fix it . . . until tonight! My whole demeanor change - I want to just smile... where I was having an anxiety attack five minutes ago on the couch is gone, and I feel safe! A fear that's been with me for three or four years now is gone! (I recommend this for anxiety) *a thousand times over!*"
- **Robert Posey**
Student, Marietta, Georgia

"I feel great . . . I feel a tremendous amount of energy and relief. Your work is very powerful!"
- Dr. Brenda Wade
TV Psychologist and Keynote Speaker
Author, *What Mama Couldn't Tell Us About Love*
www.drbrendawade.com
San Francisco, California

"I didn't know what to expect and was totally flabbergasted by this new method that removes blocks right away. I was surprised by what I found out about myself and thank Dr. Michael and his wife Brigitte for spreading the goods. I also thank the many that shared their experience for a better understanding of this new found method. A must see and most definitely must experienced for a better you!
- Brigitte Corneille
Business and Personal Coach, Atlanta

"The issue was actually some guilt I had carried around - for forty years - over the fact that I have never been able to get my daughter another good father, since her father died a month before she was born . . . and I felt like I had failed. I was really surprised that it (her Logical Soul® session) *was so simple.* I mean, I've done past life regressions, and odds and ends over the years and its all time consuming, and heart-wrenching to some degree, but this was so simple and so easy . . . and at this point I feel like I'm free from that . . . carrying that burden! I can move forward with a lighter feeling . . . just feeling more free in my relationship with my daughter."
- Linda Light
Realtor
Franklin, North Carolina

"I've read, watched, and listened to a lot of personal development content over the years. Also, I've attended many personal development events that were empowering, but The Logical Soul® incorporates all the strategies and techniques into this one book. I love how Michael makes implementing these life changing techniques easy. This is an excellent book for anyone ready to make a life change, today!"
C.F. Jackson
Author / Consultant, Atlanta, Georgia
Content Coordinator for **www.idefinetv.com**

"Gee, what . . . five minutes and there it was . . . there was an answer? The Logical Soul® is the greatest method of self-discovery I have found in my years of searching!"
- Beate Fisher
Sales Executive
Ethan Allen Furniture,
Atlanta, Georgia

"Michael's Logical Soul® method is one that very expediently identifies and reaches back to the very beginning of our emotional blocks and fear patterns that emanate from our parents and previous generations of ancestors that originated them . . . I can say without hesitation, that in my 28 years of my research I've found Michael to be one of the most compassionate, dedicated and sincere facilitators I've ever encountered."
- Lexie Ross
Writer & Journalist
Stone Mountain, Georgia

"I have learned so much from Michael . . . also from the support of the [Powerful Goals Program] group. It has been an incredible experience for me. I feel that I open up more; that I really discover my hidden decisions - that

I can go deeper and deeper every time . . . that I hit the core of the issues, and it has been just incredible. I think I am more reliable. I just feel different; [like] a different human being. I have more trust in myself, and I know I can do so many more things, what I ever have done, and it made me feel free . . . .

I recommend it to everyone because I feel it can really free your life. It can so enhance every area of your life. It's just amazing! Thank you so much from my heart for all that you are doing and creating for yourself and others."
- Birgit Blecken
Therapist
Atlanta, Georgia

"I found the work to be quietly effective in addressing sensitive emotional issues. One of the indicators that my session was productive was a notable increase in mental clarity and emotional serenity. The clarity took the form of a wave of creative inspiration. The serenity showed up as a greater capacity to just let myself be. Because of the depth of the work, I am inclined to so say that it provides a window to the soul. And, like the soul itself, this work has qualities that I would describe as magical, simple, practical, gentle and, yes, logical.
- Rudy Scarfalloto, DC
Author, *The Dance of Opposites*
Writer, teacher, chiropractor
Atlanta, Georgia

"I want to express my gratitude for sharing yourself so authentically... Your book inspired me. Thank you."
- Aline Munsch
Writer, Coach & Consultant
France

FOREWORD

Whether you're single, married, divorced, wealthy, financially challenged, unemployed, part-time employed, or a full-time homemaker, you have patterns. In fact we *all* have patterns in our lives based on **decisions** we made before our brains fully matured. These hidden decisions are still with us and determine what's going on in our lives *right now.*

When my colleague Dr. Michael Craig asked me to write a Foreword to his book, I felt deeply honored. I'm a firm believer in holistic approaches to healing and consider Michael's approach very holistic.

He works with those decisions that run us on all levels of awareness and functionality; the *body,* the *emotions,* the *mind,* and the *spirit.* I've found in my thirty years of work as a holistic psychologist that, unless we involve all four modalities, we literally do *not* have the ability to leap high enough or strongly enough to escape our old patterns. We need maximum power to establish ourselves on firm ground to allow new patterns to take hold.

Because I'm also a trained scientist, I have to also say that Michael's work penetrates to the level where we literally make changes in our brain. I started my research career studying prematurely-born Macaque monkeys at the University of Washington. At the time I was measuring visual and auditory acuity, and how it developed in prematurely-born mammals.

What my years of study in neurology taught me is that life is a neurological event. I found that at the pre-conscious level – before the brain is even half formed - we make many decisions, assessments and interpretations using this immature brain, and these can interfere mightily with our own success.

Michael's work gets access to these immature brain decisions, often as early as six months. I can tell you from my own personal work with him that six months is where I had to go to clear up some of my own deep patterns.

On the spiritual – or quantum physics - level, his work enters the realm where all energy is connected. Whether you call this level of functioning spiritual or quantum, it's the level where deep healing takes place. This level involves those factors intimately tied to us through our blood, our DNA, our ancestors, and the patterns that they passed onto us, generation to generation.

This is quite exciting to me because of my own work. I've written three books about relationships and healing, and focus on a tool called the *Genogram.* The *Genogram* looks at three generations in your family and how you can trace patterns through them. I feel Michael's work is very much in alignment with this inter-generational holistic approach.

The *Logical Soul*® is an approach that has both depth and breadth. It also begs for scientific study – a way to validate the mechanism, or how it truly affects the brain. I'd like to know more about how we can use it to change patterns in the brain, and how we can make a profound difference in the lives of those willing to take the powerful step towards this work.

I look forward to many years of working with Michael and shifting patterns in as many people as we can possibly reach. Those who have the intent to truly change their lives can, in a few short sessions, move closer indeed to profound inner shifts as I did in my own work with Michael.

What's most important to me is that we heal deeply, and understand the power that we have as human beings to shift our patterns. This, in turn, will shift the results we create in our lives, as well as transform our destiny. My entire professional life has been dedicated to this purpose.

I know that Michael is traveling this exciting journey right alongside me and many other colleagues who are doing deep holistic work. You have in your hands a great tool for change. Use it and you'll find the same benefit, the same release of energy that I felt working with Michael. I strongly encourage you to see yourself as the master of your own destiny. With Michael's work, you can, in fact, realize this mastery in your life.

Blessings on your journey,

Dr. Brenda Wade

Dr. Wade is a holistic psychologist, television host of the nationally syndicated show, "Can This Marriage be Saved?", and has been featured on Oprah, CNN, Dr. Oz, the Today Show, and Good Morning America. She is the author of three books: *Love Lessons, A Guide to*

Transforming Relationships; What Mama Couldn't Tell Us About Love; and *Power Choices: Seven Steps to Creating Wholeness, Joy, Love, and Peace.* She is also the founder of the International Love & Money Summit and offers regular advice and insights at www.drbrendawade.com.

TABLE OF CONTENTS

Publishers Data	II
About the Author	III
Dedication	IV
Testimonials	V
Foreword	IX
Introduction	1
1. Self-Sabotage: How We Manage to Not Get What We Really Want	5
Mind Magic . . . or Illusion?	
The Origin of Self-Sabotage	
"Detoxing" Mental Pollution	
Lots of What If's	
2. The World Within	15
The Good Enough Reason	
The Cycle of Manifestation	
3. Reasons Are Not Logical . . . And Logic is Not Reasonable	25
Don't Worry. Be Happy.	
Hidden Decisions Create Your Destiny	
4. The Secret of Motivation	33
Maslow's Theory	
How Spilt Motivation Arises	
The Case of Beate	
The Law of Human Reality	

5. How to Overcome the "Success Gap" And Create Anything You Want 43
    My Life of Pain
    The Quest
    Soul Logic: How It Works
    Why Most Success Courses Don't Work

6. My Search for the Source 51
    The Wisdom of the Body
    The *Real* Law of Manifestation
    You Can Direct Your Destiny

7. The Discovery of Access 59
    Cathy's Wake Up Call
    Our Conscious Handicap
    Mesmerizing Facts
    The Meaning of Soul "Logic"

8. Cartoons and Gurus: A Seeker's Guide To Hidden Decisions 67
    Looney Tunes Strikes Again
    Seal It With a Kiss
    I Feel the Earth Move
    That Guru Thing

9. The Discovery of Soul Logic 77
    Emotional Surgery Appointment
    Adventure in Sri Lanka
    Wandering in the Wilderness

10. How to Assess Your Inner Dialogue and Goal-to-Action Conflicts 85
    Why Can't We All Just Get Along?
    How to Muscle Test
    How to Self-Test
    Testing for Money Issues
    The Inner Decision-Maker

11. The Three Selves 97
    The Search for Kahuna Magic
    The Low Self
    The Middle Self
    The High Self
    How the Magic Was Lost
    Huna and The Logical Soul®

12. How to Empower Your Affirmations 109

13. How to Deal With Criticism and Failure 117
    The Feeling in Your Gut
    The Seeds of Failure (and Success)
    Failure Has a Very Good Reason
    Major Decision: Open of Closed?

14. How to Discover Your Seed of Failure 125
    The Hidden Critic
    How I Lost the Store
    Steps to Discovery

15. The Interview 131
    A Simple Technique
    Getting Started
    The Five Why's
    Begging the Question
    Testing the Statement

16. Discovery 139
    The Importance of instant Feedback
    Hey, I'm Not So Sure About This Testing...
    Using the Voice for Testing
    The Truth

17. Access 147
    What *Is* Access?
    Paradigm Surfing
    Your Personal Paradigms
    Personal Guides and Archetypes

18. Resolution 155
    Grounding Exercise
    Re-Testing
    The *Real* Law of Attraction (and a Final Note)

**19. Using the The Logical Soul®
for Effective Goal-Setting** 161
    Can't. Never Could.
    You Are Not Alone
    The Test of Time
    Patterns Can Change

**20. How to Set Benchmarks
For Effective Goal-Setting** 167
    How to Set Time Benchmarks
    How to Set Income Benchmarks
    How to Set Business Benchmarks

21. The Wall 175
    Your Private Heartbreak Hill
    Overcoming Your Private Fairy Tale
    More About Cathy
    The Un-Therapy

22. The Strange Case of Free Will 185
    The Great Debate
    Life on Cruise Control
    The Inevitable Mr. Hyde

23. Your Inner Default Settings 193
    Sometimes That's All There Is
    Organic Decisions
    The Solution
    Grace and Love
    Forms of Grace
    Changeable Defaults

24. Ritual & Taboo: A Conspiracy of Meaning .. 203
    Those Things We Do
    The Search for Meaning
    Ritual and Everyday Life
    The Third Way

25. Ancestral Decisions 213
    There's a Whole Lot of Stuff in There...
    Ancestral Influence is Strong
    Our Roots are Close to Home
    The Deepest Level of Forgiveness

26. The Power of Ancestry 221
    The Reunion Project
    Jim's Discovery

27. The Role of Intuition 229
    Our Link to the Cosmos
    Intuition and the Three Selves
    How to Invoke Intuition
    You are Destined to Be Successful!
    Viruses of the Mind

28. Your Personal Story 237
    The Kid
    No Spiders Needed
    Drop That Kryptonite!
    Variations on a Theme
    Archetypal Decisions

29. The Real Secret of How to Achieve Anything You Want in Life 247
    What Do You Really Want?
    You and Your Onion
    Overcoming Self-Deception
    Short Suffering
    Change Your Personal Story

**30. How to Create
Powerful Goals for a Lifetime** **253**
My Promise
One More Thing...

APPENDIX A **257**
How To Use the Logical Soul® Method

APPENDIX B **267**
The Logical Soul® Forgiveness Process

APPENDIX C **271**
The Logical Soul® Amends Process

FOOTNOTES **273**

INDEX **277**

INTRODUCTION

Sometimes life works in ways you don't expect.

For about ten years before the publication of the first edition of this book in 2010, my wife Brigitte (Soma) and I bought, renovated and rented out vacation properties. It seemed only logical that once I was established I should write and market books and courses based on my experiences. I even went so far as to hire some coaches to help me in this endeavor.

A few months into the process, I went on vacation to the Georgia coast. Soma and I stopped at a Taco Bell in Macon to have lunch with an old friend Ed Steeley who was one of my Meditation students back in the 1970's. During the conversation, both Ed and Soma reminded me about how the *Logical Soul*® technique had changed their lives and the lives of so many others – *often in 30 minutes or less* - and asked me why I wasn't doing this any more.

I had no answer. Suddenly all the other adventures seemed like a distraction I'd created to avoid doing my *real* work. Instantly, a new intention was born: to get this technique out to those who need and want it.

Within a month, I had written my rough draft, produced an online video series, and launched a new training course - the *Powerful Goals Program*^{tm} - with a group of eager clients that has since morphed into a newer version

The Logical Soul®

called **Logical Soul® Training** for those who are coaches and want to take this work to the next level.

Sixteen years of wandering brought me back to my true calling. The first two editions were well received, and I hope you like this third effort, updated to include some new course material.

****

The Logical Soul® is a simple, natural technique that can virtually *eliminate* self-sabotage and uncover your true passion. Using a unique method of self-inquiry, you can access and resolve *hidden decisions* that are the basic building blocks of mind viruses, and erroneous thoughts and ideas.

This method can also effectively help you
   a) *synchronize your brainwaves,*
   b) *triple your capacity* for business and income, and
   c) unleash the power to achieve any other goal you may have . . . very often in 30 minutes or less!

Any goal is only as effective as your inner clarity or intention. By becoming clear and *congruent*, your intent – and the goals that follow - will happen on all levels: mentally, emotionally, physically and *intuitively.* With a clear mind, your goals become *real* for you, and not just some abstract desire or wish.

This method, by the way, *is the real basis of the Law of Attraction!* It is a process whereby deep-rooted (subconscious) *hidden decisions* – the roots of all mind viruses, problems and self-sabotage - are discovered, accessed, and changed. We are not aware that we have or had ever made these decisions very early in our lives.

When these decisions get made, they get tucked away beyond our attention. However, we still continue to live our lives based on these decisions, even though they were made way back when we were perhaps only two or three years old. *Many decisions are not even our own,* but are inherited from ancestors, friends, relatives, teachers and religious leaders.

In order to access these *decisions,* which a lot of times are preverbal (made before you could even speak), you have to be able to ask the soul or subconscious mind – the only one who remember these decisions. *The soul remembers everything.* It really never forgot *any decision you've ever made.*

The *Logical Soul®* – with its use of a simple muscle-testing technique - is a way of accessing those decisions whether you're conscious of them or not. Consequently, there is no need for hypnosis or suggestion techniques. It is not a goal or affirmation technique – although it will strengthen the ones you use.

Using this technique involves a **4-Step Process.** With each precise step, you will learn to

- **Find** your own life's needs and destiny,
- **Discover** *Hidden Decisions* that give rise to self-sabotage and create your current reality,
- **Access** those decisions, and
- **Resolve,** "detox" and change them quickly.

This book will reveal:

- *Self-Sabotage: How We Manage to Not Get What We Really Want!* (Chapter 1)
- *The Secret of Motivation* (Chapter 4),
- *Inner Dialogue & Goal-to-Action Conflicts* (Chap 10),
- *An Ancient healing model for the mind and body* (Chapter 11),
- *How to Empower your Affirmations* (Chapter 12),

- *How to deal with Criticism and Failure* (Chapter 13),
- *Step-by-Step Instructions on how to use the Logical Soul® method* (Chapters 15-18, Appendix)
- *The role of Ancestors* (Chapters 25 & 26), and
- *How to Use Intuition* for your success! (Chapter 27)

It will also show you how to create powerful goals for a lifetime, give you some free gifts, and provide you with some unique bonuses and an opportunity to achieve your goals at will.

True knowledge comes from within, not imposed from the outside. Once you tap into those memory sources, you will *just know.* That's the beauty of the whole process – the process that I will reveal in this book through stories and case studies.

Enjoy the stories. Enjoy the explanations. But most of all enjoy the feeling of freedom you will have once you tap into some of that old hidden "stuff" and watch self-sabotage dissolve through the power of the *Logical Soul®*!

CHAPTER ONE

Self-Sabotage: How We Manage to *NOT Get* What We Really Want!

"You never change things by fighting the existing reality. To change something, build a new model that makes the existing model obsolete."
- R. Buckminster Fuller

Mind *Magic* . . . or Illusion?

Have written goals.

These words bounced between my ears during a decade of soul-searching. It started in 1985 after a devastating blow – the loss of a girlfriend by suicide.

I was looking for answers. Positive motivation. Clear thinking. An easy and fast way to find and achieve goals. What I *really* needed was a lifeline to pull me from the sea of despair I had fallen into – and I needed one fast.

Friends tried to help. They informed me that **Dr. David Schwartz,** author of *The Magic of Thinking Big* would be speaking at the Church of Life Science that Saturday in downtown Atlanta. I was not feeling up to it, but forced myself nevertheless to attend. I figured I could always come back to my suffering and pity-party later.

What I saw and heard changed my life. Dr. Schwartz reached into my soul and pulled out a nugget of pure life. I really perked up that day. *Finally* here was someone who could help me. Here at last was my lifeline!

Each page of *Magic* was true to its words. Turning page after page I became delirious with hope and optimism. Chills of excitement arose in a huge crescendo of life and love. For the first time in many years I felt I had *a clear direction in life* . . . one that would positively affect my life and the lives of others. I wanted to arise from the ashes and be like Dr. Schwartz.

I wanted success in all its forms so badly that I could taste it, feel it, touch it, smell it. Over the next several months and years I loaded up on books and tapes by other positive motivational writers, speakers and trainers: Ziglar, Wattles, Hill, Butterworth, Rohn, Robbins, Canfield and dozens more. I couldn't get enough of them. I wanted to drive out every negative thought I had ever had and replace them with positive, loving, powerful and dynamic thoughts, affirmations and goals. I wanted it all!

And I DID succeed. I was able to eliminate many of my self-destructive tendencies, find a wonderful woman who became my second wife, take a 5-month trip to Asia, greatly expand my knowledge and healing abilities, and establish friendships that have lasted to this day. I also got my sense of humor back and began to feel better about just being ME.

What I was NOT able to do, however, was to achieve financial success. "Thinking big" had done little to advance my wealth goals and objectives. I still lacked the ability to break through and attract money into my life. Oh, I HAD my written goals alright. I had written *"I joyfully earn and accept over a million dollars in income per year"* and fully planned to have this be my reality by age 35. Then it got extended to age 40. Then 45. Then 50 . . .

Yet it didn't happen. In spite of the fact that I had written my goals down over and over again daily, it didn't happen. In spite of all attempts to re-program my mind, it didn't happen.

In the beginning I had even gone so far as to record an audiotape - with Mozart music in the background – repeating every one of my goals and affirmations. I listened to this tape whenever I could during the day, and even programmed a timer to turn on the tape at night to play into a speaker under my pillow. Then something happened: I lost a lot of sleep and had to discontinue this exercise. Other than that? Zilch. Zero. Nada.

Years later I finally figured out the main reason for this lapse of magic and my failure to taste success. It was _my own powerful hidden agendas_ that kept me from taking *effective* action, getting results, and staying broke.

Dr. Schwartz had failed to take into account that my magnetic attraction to *NOT* having money was *so* pervasive, *so* persistent and *so* deep that all the affirmations in the world could not change that. Even though I had stuck to the program religiously and practically eliminated blame and excuses from my world – what Schwartz calls "Excusitis." Still, nothing worked.

I certainly *felt* better, but my outside reality didn't really shift all that much. No excuses. Just facts.

I had stumbled across the "open secret" that eluded me for years – that <u>conscious thought and desire is only the tip of the iceberg.</u> I discovered that for every little *Kon-Tiki* raft which makes it across the ocean, there are 96 or more that never do. By eliminating "Excusitis" I was able to at least stumble across this knowledge honestly – even if it did take me twenty years!

The Gift

There was a hidden power within me that was "on" to all my goals, programs, affirmations, and other tricks I could throw at it. This power would meet my challenge and exceed it. This power represented **decisions** made when I was very young that were <u>dedicated to my survival</u> in this world, and *nothing* could dislodge it. Not even the elimination of *Excusitis*.

This power was the true *origin* of my toxic mind, more commonly known as **self-sabotage,** or the conflict between my conscious and subconscious decisions that kept my mind bogged down.

I was dealing with a type of *mental pollution* that kept me constantly at odds with myself . . . and that without "detoxing" my mind I would remain stuck. Outwardly I felt like a failure, but according to my *inner* programming, I was not a failure at all. This apparent paradox was the problem I was up against, i.e., a wall that separated my conscious and subconscious motivation for success.

But how could I bridge such a wall? Change such a formidable power? The first step, I figured, was to determine the extent of this hidden foe. What was I was up against?

The Origin of Self-Sabotage

"Self-sabotage" manifests itself in the phenomenon of *split purpose.* You say you will do something that is really important in your life, like losing ten pounds; then you proceed to *take every action possible to AVOID losing those ten pounds.* But why would you do that?

Obviously, there is another mind – a hidden one – that has a completely different agenda from the one our conscious mind selected. We all know this; that's why we tend to claim "the devil made me do it," or treat the body as some kind of child having a tantrum at our expense.

What we DON'T realize, however, is that the body and subconscious have a **"prime directive"** to survive at all cost. If that means holding on to those ten pounds then, by golly, it will do that! The fact that you don't truly understand or appreciate this fact is of little consequence. You will, just the same, be held hostage by the force that seeks survival.

Less obviously, survival issues enter into things we would think have nothing to do with it.

Let's say you sabotage your chances of success by not accepting gifts and money when offered. Wouldn't survival dictate that you get as much stuff as possible? Not necessarily. The "logic of the soul" remembers your father who lectured you about accepting money as a small child. He told you it "wasn't polite." Fear of the father (i.e., survival) led you to believe, therefore, that gifts were dangerous.

Self-Sabotage simply means *our minds are polluted by survival decisions* made as small children that continue to interfere with our success as adults. This "mind toxicity" creates the need to negate ideas and resources we might otherwise embrace and accept.

"Detoxing" Mental Pollution

If we do indeed suffer from *mental pollution,* how can we *"detox"* our minds? How do we get rid of this sticky problem??

"Pollution" said the great inventor and futurist **R. Buckminster Fuller,** *"is nothing but the resources we are not harvesting. We allow them to disperse because we've been ignorant of their value."*[1]

Pollution is, basically, useful material that we consider trash because we see no use for it. Take, for example the emission of sulphur fumes from smokestacks. Pollution, right? Yes, to those who breathe the air.

But to a chemist involved in manufacturing sulphur compounds, drugs, explosives, fungicides, and other materials, this same "pollutant" is a valuable element. If those who breathe the air *knew* this – *and* if there were a way to cost-effectively capture the sulphur from these same smokestacks – everyone would suddenly applaud sulphur as a magical Godsend.

Similarly, *mental pollution* is the manifestation of certain thoughts, feelings and ideas that we interpret as mind chatter, fear, envy, resentment and consider it the voice of restriction, doom and failure. We *think* these are negative thought forms simply because they run contrary to our conscious needs and desires. This belief is reinforced by a vast army of motivational speakers and teachers telling us to ignore this *"stinkin' thinkin'"* and cultivate the habit of staying positive.

Positive thinking, however, has its limitations. These underlying things called "reality" and "logic" keep getting in the way.

> *"If generic 'positive thought' is correct and things are really getting better; if the arc of the universe tends towards happiness and abundance, then why bother with the mental effort of positive thinking? Obviously, because we do not believe that things will get better on their own. The practice of positive thinking is*

an effort to pump up this belief in the face of much contradictory evidence . . . it requires deliberate self-deception, including a constant effort to repress or block out unpleasant possibilities and 'negative thoughts'. . ."[2]

Indeed, the idea of positive thinking has become so ingrained (in American culture particularly) that your first thoughts of the concept of "mental detox" may have been that it is *another way to get rid of negative thoughts,* right? If so, you have probably tried to root out your own negativity in a variety of ways. Most such methods are not effective.

Mental pollution, just like the so-called polluting sulphur produced by smoke stacks, has its benefits. These benefits simply cannot be recognized because you want something and this "negative thought" stands in your way.

Lots of What If's

What if this so-called "negative" thought was actually your own subconscious trying desperately to feed you a message? What if this message went something like this:

> "Hey you! That's right – YOU - the one with that stupid grin on your face trying to ignore me! Give me a minute, will ya? I'm dying down here and all you can do is pile more dirt and crap on top of me. Hey, you know what? Because you keep doing that, I'm going to throw the crap right back at ya.
>
> That's right. No more Mr.(Ms.) Nice Guy . . . remember that important meeting you missed

because I made you play video games until you forgot to leave the house? Yeah, that one. That contract could have netted us a small fortune. Remember that eating habit you have that put on 30 pounds? Me again. But you know what? I don't give a gnat's ass what happens because of the way you keep ignoring my messages. You're probably not listening to this one either. Think I'll make us trip over that rug . . . !"*

What if your silent *subconscious mind* could actually learn how to speak to you and give it to you straight without all the not-so-subtle hints? Would you listen? If not, you're missing a whale of a chance to succeed BIG in this world. . and to be much happier in the process!

So what if you think you failed in the past, and don't want to listen to this so-called "voice of failure." This voice – a part of your soul - is trying to give you the LOGIC behind his or her voice. If you don't choose to hear that, you have failed before you start, just like I did multiple times.

Bucky Fuller revealed *"I only learn what to do when I have failures."* [3]

A *mental detox* is simply a way of actually *getting access to* and *listening to* your own voice within . . . then changing certain *hidden decisions* and allowing a *natural resolution* to take place. It is much simpler than you think, and will allow you to discover a whole new world of possibilities!

The Logical Soul®

CHAPTER TWO

The World Within

"Our power is in our ability to decide."
- R. Buckminster Fuller

The Good-Enough Reason

How would you like to be able to detox your mind and have pretty much everything you want . . . **in 30 minutes or less?**

Yeah, I know. This is in the title and sounds a little crazy, right? It is . . . but maybe not for the reasons you think.

You see, most people believe *it takes a long time* to realize success. I did. I set my goals to be achieved within five years. Then I fought for them, seeking to overcome any inner resistance and negativity. It didn't work.

Like me, others who are serious about success also have written goals to achieve it, along with daily affirmations. They visualize their success, work, slave, toil and sweat... and by the end of the day, month or several years they figure they will reap the reward.

In this world, success or reward usually _does_ take a long time. Telling people they could have it in thirty minutes or less will only get you blank stares, disbelief . . . or laughter.

This happens because most of us understand that the world of the tried-and-true success formula will work well only IF we can stick with it! Alas! Nobody realizes that this is where the written goals and hard work *really* comes in, i.e., maintaining the **persistence** necessary to complete all the action steps for long-term success.

Persistence is something I had trouble with as a child and as a young adult. Like many others my age I had this mistaken idea that *anything* could happen if I wished for it strongly enough. *Santa Claus* proved that it happened. So did Peter Pan and the Tooth Fairy. Most fairy tales showed that magic was all you needed in order to turn thread into gold and weave an invisible cloth! Wow! What a world!

As a young boy, I believed in the **"Santa Claus Theory of Reality"** which looked something like this:

Desire  Results

Life was simple, fast, and dependable. Want something? Ask Santa. He may not bring it, but he did often enough to make the yearly cycle part of our inner reality. Just the HOPE of having that magic toy, or even a *better* one next year, was enough to keep us going.

We wanted and expected everything to be available instantly. As kids, we hadn't yet experienced the "hard knocks" our parents so often talked about. Work? Persistence? Why bother?

Those who *were* persistent – like Ebenezer Scrooge (no Christmas spirit) Wile E. Coyote (too stupid), and my Dad (too grumpy) – paid for theirs with much pain and suffering. Day-to-day business seemed to me so boring! If I couldn't manifest it within days, weeks or a month, I'd move on to the next thing. I guess I didn't have many role models there to choose from.

I suspect MOST people lack persistence when talking about things they *say* they want. After realizing the effort, willpower and struggle required, most of us give up. There are, in fact, *very few goals* that give us a **good enough reason** to persist. Oddly enough, the struggle is mostly *internal* . . . but we'll get to that later.

The Logical Soul® shows us a world that is hidden and powerful – one that can light up our imagination, bring back our willpower, and generate solid persistence . . . *naturally!* This power, however, can cut both ways. Learning how to navigate in it takes tremendous focus and dedication. No wimps allowed!

The world I speak of has to do with BEING, not doing. This is the world deep inside us – so deep, in fact, you may consider it to be our "soul" or the unseen power that enlivens our body and motivates our every thought and action.

Your Soul is the *essence* of who you really are. It CAN manifest anything you truly want . . . inside. Even in five minutes. Even in a *nano-second.*

The Cycle of Manifestation

Unless you already have a big staff working out all the details, the *Santa Claus Theory* doesn't work. Depending on the strength of your innermost thoughts and desires, your results will either be

   a) strong and focused, or
   b) weak and scattered.

If your Soul is in turmoil, your results will also be similar. Conversely, if your Soul or Being is *dynamic, strong* and *clear,* the resulting thoughts, actions and achievements will be also dynamic, strong and clear.

Assuming you are strong and clear, your *INSIDE* (thoughts and desires) will naturally express itself through your ability to manifest *OUTSIDE* (Results).

The process flows simply and directly from *thought* to *action* to *fulfillment,* and would look like the **normal cycle** below . . .

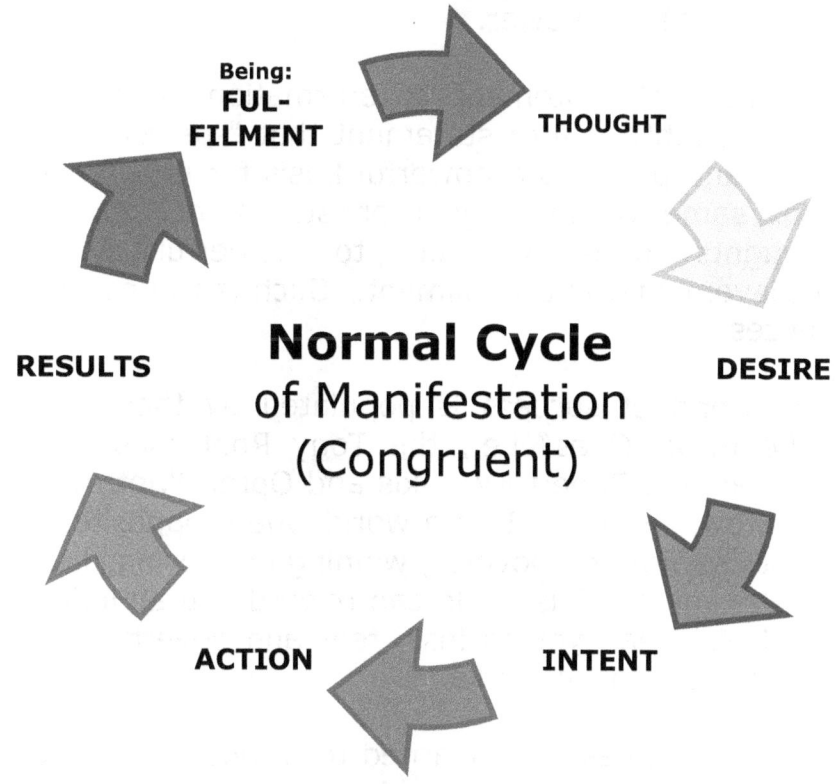

The above flow from *Being* and *Thought* to *Action* and *Results* has only two outcomes. Either it **a)**

The Logical Soul®

lines up with our conscious DESIRE and INTENT, or **b)** fights it.

If both our inner (subconscious) desire/intent and external (conscious) desire/intent are in alignment with one another, I call them *congruent*.

Congruent intentions are ones that resonate positively on all levels: mentally, emotionally, physically and spiritually. There comes an "inner knowing" that automatically translates into external results. Successful people naturally have (or have developed) this power.

A congruent statement or affirmation is therefore any thought, goal or statement that *"speaks to your soul"* and provides a powerful basis for *fulfillment* of that same thought, goal or statement. Powerful thoughts naturally lead to powerful actions, achievements, and fulfillment. Such is the nature of success.

The world of success is populated by those I call *"The Great Ones"* i.e., the Tony Robbinses, David Schwartzes, Robert Kyosakis and Oprah Winfreys we all know and love. It is a world where opposites co-exist: wealth and poverty, winning and losing; health and sickness. This world can reward you abundantly OR it can lead you to loss, fear and poverty IF you don't know how it works.

The Great Ones have learned to navigate within this world effortlessly by becoming congruent or *aligned with their real intent.* They naturally **focus** on what they want and **conceive** of owning it *right now*, not months or years later. While it may take longer to arrive physically, the object of their intention has already been manifested . . . much like ordering a gift item over the phone and giving them your credit card details. It is done. Move on to the next item.

Once Oprah Winfrey decides to have a person on as a guest, this person becomes a wealthy overnight celebrity. When Tony Robbins chooses to have perfect health, he not only finds a way to bring it about, he enrolls *thousands* of other people into this idea as well! Such is the raw power of congruent intent, or clear focus.

Hidden decisions, on the other hand, create **errors, self-sabotage,** and *incongruent* **intentions.** Mixed intentions simply fight one another and waste energy, life, and results.

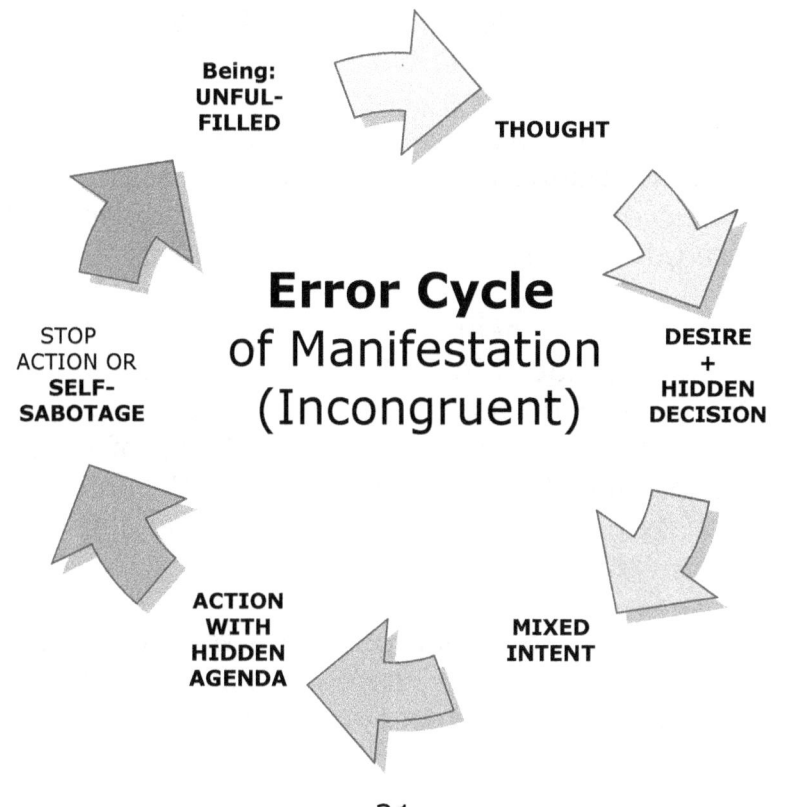

There is no "inner knowing" since there is little connection between with the real source of one's power and the ability to express it. These folks – the vast majority of humans, by the way – stumble through life and are never able to quite "get it together." They remain unfulfilled, as shown in the following diagram . . .

Even the Great Ones experience power that cuts both ways. A recent example is the champion golfer Tiger Woods. Once he dials up a Birdie on the fourth hole in Augusta, there's little doubt he will get it. But decisions in his personal life nearly destroyed him. Such is the raw power of intent . . . or mixed intent!

Pursuing the Tiger story further, we can also see that intent must be coupled with **integrity;** otherwise we can potentially crash and burn.

Loss of integrity can give rise to both hidden and conscious decisions that may turn out to be deadly to our success. Once Intent and Integrity are both mastered, however, the world is ours.

Integrity simply means alignment with both our inside and outside. Integrity is *authenticity.* Since Mr. Woods allowed us to perceive him as this clean-cut family man, his womanizing caught us off-guard. His actions were like a bullhorn blast in the middle of a church hymn, i.e., insulting. His actions didn't jive with his message; ergo, lack of integrity.

Stars like Mick Jagger and Elvis, on the other hand, were *perceived* as a chronic party-goers and womanizers . . . and most fans didn't care. Their actions as rock stars *were congruent with their message* and we loved them all the more for it!

So how do the Great Ones master these characteristics and develop such focus? My guess is they were born with it, then nurtured by an environment that strengthened their genius. If you believe in reincarnation, you might even suggest they earned it!

That does not mean, however, there is no hope for the rest of us. There is, indeed, a way to develop the same **success instinct** – one decision at a time.

CHAPTER THREE

Reasons are Not Logical... and Logic is Not Reasonable

"It's only in the mysterious equations of love can logic and reason truly be found."
- John Nash, upon accepting the
Nobel Prize in Mathematics in 1994

Don't Worry. Be Happy.

I asked a few of those who I consider *the Great Ones* how they achieved success, and they told me: "Focus on what you are passionate about, and use that **burning desire** to take action and see it through to completion."

This advice is simple, to-the-point, and accurate. It was also of *very little help* to me and maybe 96% of the human population.

You see, we tend to filter out success talk, even when it is repeated over and over again. The Seed of Failure is so strong – and so insidious – that even though we may intellectually understand and seek out/ try to find/hunt for a "burning desire" and action, yet the nervous impulse from that desire somehow gets lost in the maze of inner turmoil!

I know. I persisted in following "success formulae" for *decades* and never got anywhere. Pumped-up motivation was never able to push through my inner chaos, and I usually gave up out of sheer exhaustion.

Oh, I had great intentions, but they were neither strong nor long-lasting. Inner, *hidden decisions* had sabotaged the outcomes. It took more than intention to break through my mediocrity.

Even the Great Ones know this. In listening to conversations between very successful people,[1] where there is a sincere intention/intent to lift others up and share their bounty, but they know they must usually settle for those 4% of people who will *actually make something happen* in their lives. They know that most people lead lives of quiet desperation and will never see the light of success shine through.

Do they have regrets? Not really. Some sadness? Yes. After all, most of them give us everything they have. They even outline the same steps they themselves used to succeed, and would be tickled pink if we followed in their footsteps! But the law of averages – and hidden decisions – block our receptiveness to their message.

The Great Ones have shown us how they manifest at will from a level of being that is congruent on all levels: mentally, physically, and emotionally. They have also given us valuable techniques to develop sharp focus, and stay on course.

They are not equipped, however, to show us - the ordinary folk - HOW to step into the *same congruent state* they are in, deep inside. *Until we change that crucial inner decision to NOT join them,* we will always be looking in from the outside.

Part of the problem is that *they* see us as being like *them*. To them, we are just successful people waiting to discover some success habits, tools, methods or motivation. It's only natural that those who are successful would expect to see the world populated with people like themselves, i.e., successful and happy. Consequently, they don't *grasp the full extent* of our subconscious *will to fail . . .* or simply refuse to acknowledge it.

To put it another way, they don't see how we "succeed" in a much different way than they do.

We lose money, choose the wrong businesses, get cheated and abused, and basically live a life full of drama and suffering because our hidden idea of "success" means that we are well on our way to our secret goal, i.e., gradual self-destruction.

This kind of success, however, is only logical to our subconscious mind. While it may seem very *illogical* to stay unmotivated, poor, scattered and angry, our subconscious motivation sees this as a perfect solution to the hidden decisions we have set in motion.

The Great Ones, however, can only teach from where they are, i.e., *already congruent and motivated inside!* They already have that *"fire in the belly"* but can't give it to us. They can talk about it through words, paint us a picture, or teach us techniques, but cannot *walk our path for us*.

They even tell us this. Not having their deep congruence and confidence, however, we continue to fail . . . that is until we discover the way to transform the same drive for failure into a drive for success.

Asking some Great Ones to teach us how to transform this drive and get congruent is like asking them to teach us how to breathe! Such a basic human trait! They figure that their field is *success,* not therapy . . . and that people who can't get congruent probably need more of the latter.

Mozart considered himself a composer, and usually rejected requests to teach more basic stuff, like playing piano . . .

> *"I leave that to people who cannot do anything but play the piano. I am a composer,"* he wrote to his mother in 1778. **4**

To the Great Ones, developing a burning desire for higher levels of existence and creation is such a basic idea they don't really understand the problem. Basic instruction? Yes, it is needed. But once proficiency is attained and all the motivational techniques absorbed, they reason, why would *anyone* be lacking the *drive* to succeed . . . unless of course they were lazy?

The Logical Soul®

To their credit, however, most successful motivators love teaching and never stop putting it out there. For those ready to receive these pearls of wisdom, the seeds they plant take root and grow. For those not ready, they still did the best they could.

By the way, one of the reasons for the success of the Great Ones is because of their tremendous powers of **persuasion.** While in their presence you believe in yourself, even if you never did before. They rub off on you. Their enthusiasm, use of key phrasing, and ability to weave stories into their message, give us all hope and vision. You walk out of the room feeling ten feet tall!

However, it doesn't last. Unless they are willing to watch over your shoulders day after day, week after week, <u>and personally guide you</u> until you succeed, their lessons are usually forgotten the next day. Or next week. The motivation is usually gone before it can make a real difference in our thought and action patterns and habits. Then we are right back where we started: frustrated and poor.

Most Great Ones were born with an innate talent to see success everywhere they go. A successful friend of mine calls this talent "Money Goggles" and says that all successful people see the world through a different filter compared to those who consistently fail.

But the instructions seldom change in their basic message: write down your goals, set benchmarks, tap your shoulder or head, and anchor your beliefs.

Fake it 'til you make it. Act successful so you will *BE* successful. Start seeing success in everything you do, and in all things surrounding you. . .

Sound advice, but we fail anyway. We fail because our inner perception of ourselves is that we can't "get it," learn it or keep it, even when it's given to us. We think we are too stupid, too lazy, or a combination of any of these.

So we think the solution is to replace the negative thoughts with more positive ones. I did. The more I tried to throw positive thoughts into my mind, however, the more negative I became deep inside. There was an inner contradictory power that kicked in the moment I tried to consciously take over. *I was digging my own grave with positive thinking!*

The simple truth is, while we desperately want to emulate the Great Ones, the harder we try, the more we seem to fail. And they cannot comprehend how complicated and convoluted our sabotaging hidden decisions are, nor can they teach us to UN-complicate them!

Hidden Decisions Create Your Destiny

Don't get me wrong. I never said the Great Ones haven't experienced hard times. Quite the contrary: they may have had MORE tough breaks! These tough breaks and hard times, however, gave them access to an even *GREATER burning desire* than they had before! The inner, hidden decisions they made early in life gave them the strength to weather these misfortunes in such a way as to come out ahead, just as these same hidden decisions *forcefully sabotage* the rest of us.

Quite simply, a focused, burning desire cannot be learned or imparted. It must be ingrained in us from early on and *lived* from a level of being that very few understand or achieve. <u>Even the Great Ones themselves can't teach this to us!</u>

Let's take money issues as an example.

If it is wealth you want, the roadmap has already been laid out. If you do nothing but read Dr. Schwartz's <u>The Magic of Thinking Big</u> or Napoleon Hill's classic <u>Think and Grow Rich</u>, you will have *all the information you need* to be successful in *any* field:

"What the mind can conceive and believe, it can achieve."

This says it all. In fact, I used this quote to help me through some of the darkest days of my life, and it is still the primary affirmation in my life. What I discovered recently, however, was that most of us take the words "mind" and "believe" in a fundamentally different way than the Great Ones do.

Once I came to understand this difference, *I discovered the key to unlocking the secret* that keeps even the Great Ones from imparting their wisdom to others.

You see, *the Great Ones believe, from deep within themselves, they are successful.* Even in their darkest hours they KNOW this to be true, and are of ONE mind in this belief. Most humans, however, live their lives with a **split mind** – one mind conscious, the other subconscious. Consequently, their beliefs and intentions are also split.

Most of us, quite literally, are torn between desires that keep us from staying focused long enough to be successful.

CHAPTER FOUR

The Secret of Motivation

"Today is just a good day in disguise."
- Paul Venghaus

Why do we always want to *"get more motivation?"* Why can't we simply accomplish what we set out to do? Why do we always seem to lack "willpower"... and persist in chasing the idea that some magic elixir called "motivation" will cure what ails us?

I'm glad you asked.

Maslow's Theory

In 1943, a pioneer in the filed of Psychology - **Abraham H. Maslow** – published some findings that forever altered the way many psychologists and psychiatrists saw their patients. Before Maslow, psychology was primarily concerned with diseases of the mind, i.e., how the mind became sick and disorderly; psychotic or neurotic. After Maslow, the term "self-actualization" became a part of our modern vocabulary.

A *"self-actualized person"* was one who is doing what he or she does best. They are happy and loving. They get along with others in their work and at home. They solve problems. They exhibit no abnormal tendencies or neurotic stress symptoms. Their basic needs, in fact, have been fulfilled.

According to Maslow, however, there were other needs that had to be satisfied before Self-actualization could become a reality. He revealed a total of five levels of need in his **Theory of Motivation** that he published in *Psychology Review*.[5] Simply put, one could not rise in the pyramid to the next level of need until he or she had satisfied the one before it:

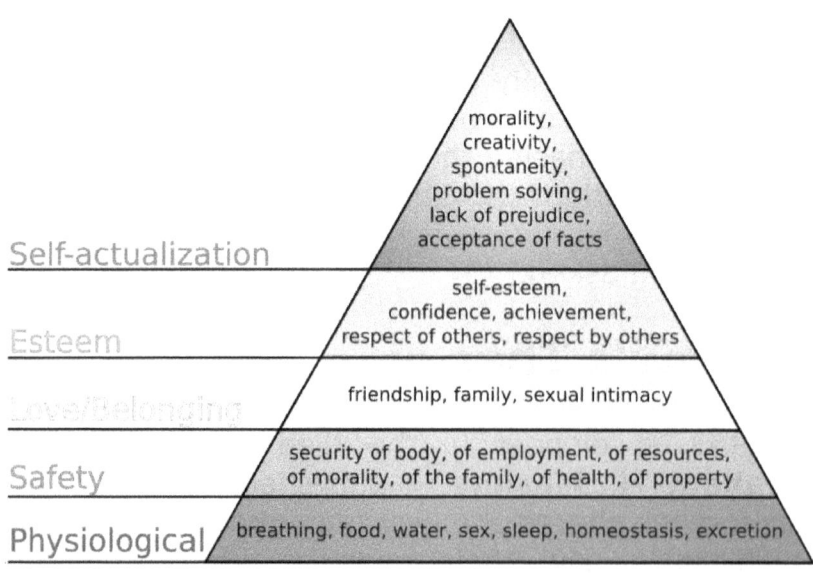

Image source: http://en.wikipedia.org

These needs are usually self-evident. Given a choice between satisfying a need like doing a job one loves (level 5) or eating (level 1), all relatively sane people will choose the latter. Its only when the need for food is satisfied does the need to have other things arise. Until then, the primary needs control.

This proves that jumping higher within the pyramid does not work. While you may try to deny a basic need in favor of a higher one, your subconscious mind will always choose the more basic as default. If you try to skip a level, self-sabotage will stop you every time.

Recently, others have added to Maslow's **Hierarchy of Needs,**[6] but his original model is the classic source for understanding human motivation.

How Split Motivation Arises

In *Logical Soul®* methodology, a "split mind" refers to a conflict between subconscious and conscious needs, and how the more basic need (i.e., "hidden decision") controls.

For example, let's say your goal is to achieve great things in life (Level 4), but have a *hidden decision* that you will *never* betray your loving Grandmother (Level 2 – security, family) who considered money as "the root of all evil." Given a choice, your nervous system will default to Level 2; this basic need must be satisfied before you can move upwards.

Given the above scenario, we are caught between *desire* and *obligation; fear* and *longing.* The decisions that govern each level arise from different parts of our brains and nervous system, giving rise to a "split" that often keeps us frozen and unable to act effectively.

This split-brain phenomenon manifests itself even in a resting brain and shows up as a slight asymmetry in **EEG studies.** Brain wave measurements performed over the past thirty years on TM (Transcendental Meditation) meditators, for example, showed that the so-called "higher" states of consciousness differ significantly from the normal electrical wave patterns found in waking, sleeping, and dreaming states and in comparisons between resting brains of meditators and non-meditators.[7]

Since some subject meditators also exhibited qualities that Maslow described as "self-actualized,"[8] it is interesting to note the variations in EEG wave patterns. The non-mediator resting brain shows a mild asymmetry, while the resting brain of a TM meditator was consistently synchronous or symmetrical.

The congruence between **right brain feelings,** wholeness and memories and **left brain logic** also becomes apparent after *Logical Soul®* sessions. While there are not yet any scientific studies to show this coherence as in TM, hundreds of positive anecdotal evidence from patients and clients indicate this could also be a rich field for research and study.

The *Logical Soul®,* in fact, was guided and developed using the same underlying principle that marked the development of TM. **Maharishi Mahesh Yogi,** the founder of TM,[9] spoke often of the basis of his technique:

"The nature of the mind is to go towards greater and greater fields of happiness that happens at finer and finer levels of the thinking process, towards the Source of Thought." [10]

Similarly, the nature of the mind during a *Logical Soul®* session is to find the path of least resistance *towards more and more happiness,* and eventually come to a state of deepest resolution (rest). The relief that most clients feel after a session is similar to that felt after a period of deep meditation.

The question then arises: If the mind is naturally drawn to resolution, WHY does it choose struggle and inner conflict?

The answer, again, lies in understanding Maslow's hierarchy of needs and how our subconscious mind must first resolve its own **default priorities** before moving on to what it considers to be lesser priorities. This "dynamic tension" between inner resolution and outer desire manifests as a personal struggle within the individual.

I became aware of my own tendency towards struggle and split awareness during my times of divorce, business failure, bankruptcy, and ill health.
I experienced a loss of inner coordination, and often felt unsettled, angry, overwhelmed, and was unable to fully communicate or express myself.
Interestingly, this condition has been described by stroke victims, i.e., the onset of different sets of inner values, loss of coordination, and other symptoms.

Dr. Jill Taylor, a noted brain scientist, experienced a left-hemispheric stroke herself, and wrote about her experiences, transformation and recovery in *A Stroke of Insight.*[11] In describing the unique onset of right-brain dominance, she discovered values that she didn't know she had. She said it became vitally important to retain her right-brain "wholeness" in spite of efforts by therapists to rehabilitate her more "logical" left brain. She was not, she said, willing to *"compromise new insights in the name of recovery."*[12]

I experienced this same, innate stubbornness myself. The hidden part of me steadfastly held onto the feeling of wholeness and meditation . . . *even if that meant giving up my financial goals in life!*

Incredible? I thought so too. This power was SO strong within me that it rendered effective action impossible.

Have you also experienced this split motivation? If you have, you understand the tremendous power that the subconscious wields over our lives, and how often it governs by default.

If you haven't experienced what I'm talking about, that does NOT mean you are free and clear. Here is a simple test: look around you. Are you successful? If so, how does this success manifest itself? Where's the proof?? What are the benchmarks you've achieved?

If you are not successful, be honest with yourself. Even if you feel some anger or resentment towards this suggestion of lack, you may be sure that your mind is split, and there are a few subtle brain waves floating around in there and *not* supporting your conscious desires.

Regardless of your state of mind, when you are ready to re-set your subconscious default to "congruent," your internal motivation will become a powerhouse of expression and manifestation. Like magic, people and resources will show up that defy all conscious logic – and yet it happens.

The Case of Beate

During the interview in a morning LS session in February, 2009, Beate reported having a life-long problem with her teeth. She had suffered horribly as a child since her teeth were considered to be in poor condition and the dentist in Germany often worked on her without administering Novocain.

During the latest session, I found a link to her mother (who also had bad teeth) and got access to change the "ancestral decision" that was in place. Beate felt instantly relief after only a few minutes and left the session very relaxed. Later she called me all excited:

> "I can't believe it!" she gushed. "The dentist said my teeth were perfectly healthy and didn't need anything. . ! I didn't expect that at all!"

Coincidence? Maybe. But such seemingly drastic changes happen all the time with the *Logical Soul®*.

The Law of Human Reality

What is your *gut* telling you about the world around you? Is it mostly about you and your responsibilities? Or is it primarily about "them" and "their faults"?

If you take responsibility for your life and acknowledge that you have a lot to do with how your world creates itself around you, *congratulations!* While you may yet have "stuff" to work on, there are no barriers to miracles happening in your life on a regular basis.

If, on the other hand, you feel like a victim and can't see how to get out of this vicious cycle, don't worry. There may be more to look at, but it's certainly not fatal. How do I know? I was stuck there myself not so very long ago!

The only thing I would ask of you (if you feel you are a victim) is to <u>*try on the idea of being responsible for everything around you.*</u> Just like you might try on a new coat, try on this idea. Even if it doesn't feel right, try it on. Humor me; you won't be sorry.

Ready? Here goes . . .

Let's pretend that the **"Law of Human Reality"** is as follows:

Your world IS what you decide - inside.

This is simply another way of repeating that New Age admonition *"The world is as you are"* <u>with one critical difference</u>. I added "inside" to decisions because that element is the *pivotal point of manifestation.* I'm not simply talking about *conscious* decisions. It's your *hidden ones* that either support or suppress ALL levels of your mind and being!

If the *Law of Human Reality* is true and operational in my life, it therefore stands to reason that I made my own inner (hidden) decisions to fail each time.

This decision – and others like it - are by definition "subconscious" and therefore could not be corrected by my *conscious intent* alone. Once set in motion, however, hidden decisions had the power to blossom into what I expected, i.e., financial failure.

So how does this apply to your life?

Do you <u>know for certain</u> that you can achieve a certain goal? In other words, *does every decision arising from within your body, mind, emotions, memory and intuition* support this goal? If so, the outcome will happen easily, quickly, and with little or no resistance.

If not, you will struggle.

And you are not alone. Look around you – lots of folks are struggling, have always struggled, and always *will* struggle. Despite the fact that the Great Ones throughout the centuries have shown us step-by-step **how** to find and keep financial and other types of success, *we continue to struggle and fail.*

The Great Ones show us how to
- conceive the concept of success,
- write it down,
- bathe in it,
- affirm it,
- visualize it, and
- live it.

We fail some more.

The Great Ones give us everything-

- The best road maps and
- The best tools!

We *still* fail.

Is it because we're stupid?   No.

Because we don't follow directions? Maybe.

Because we don't stick to it? Getting warmer . . .

Or is it because -- deep down – there is a **very good reason NOT to succeed?**

Bingo.

CHAPTER FIVE

How to Overcome the "Success Gap" and Create Anything You Want

*"If at first you don't succeed,
find out if the loser gets anything."*
- Bill Lyon

My Decade of Pain

My life, although never a bed or roses, was particularly painful in the 1980's. During that decade I experienced "more than my fair share" of pain i.e., separation, divorce, several changes of address, homelessness, poverty, sickness and the sudden death of loved ones.

All these experiences – painful as they were – gave me great inner strength. They transformed my life into a life dedicated to finding answers for what I saw was an inner *commitment* to suffering.

I just couldn't figure out *how* or *why* this was! I knew *consciously* I never wanted to suffer. Why then would I *subconsciously* crave such a fate? This riddle alone was my biggest challenge – not knowing WHAT made me do the things that made my life suck. So I set out to find a solution.

The Quest

I must've read Napoleon Hill's book a dozen times in the 1980s and 90s, and tried everything for 30 years -- meditation, goal setting, affirmations, motivational seminars, NLP, tapping, and self hypnosis. While I made significant progress, deep down within me I *still* considered myself a failure.

It wasn't until I stumbled across a very important method of getting **ACCESS** to the hidden logic of the subconscious that I began to find out WHY I failed and HOW to start untangling the horrid mess I'd made to that point. The *decisions* I made about money and success were *so strong* they erased any attempt I made to override them. YEARS of affirmations and positive self-talk had been mostly fruitless.

I simply could NOT fool this inner wisdom and resolve. All I could do was accept it, and begin to listen to the REAL REASONS why things *are* the way they are.

Once I actually discovered -- and changed -- the hidden decisions contrary to my success, *real* success was assured! I call this method of self-discovery, access and resolution the *Logical Soul®*.

Soul Logic: How It Works

The *Logical Soul®* is a simple, natural method based on the idea that at some point there was

1. **A conscious decision** made, and this decision was
2. **Burned into your consciousness** with high emotion, much like a software program or song is burned into a CD.

This deeper, ***emotion-survival-based decision*** has tremendous power -- so much so that most psychologists argue these inner programs form our worldview and are permanent. The fact is they only *appear* to be permanent, since most of the decisions on which they are based were our pre-verbal survival decisions.

To make matters *more* complicated, many inner decisions are considered to be instinctual because they pertain to the primal brain and basic bodily functions. Yet these decisions also affect the outcomes of everything we do. In fact, there are anywhere *from* **1 to 100 trillion decisions** *made every second* that affect us in ways we will never consciously understand! [13]

Although we may not understand, we are still familiar with the results. Remember the tightness in the pit of your stomach when you had to:

- Climb a tall ladder?
- Meet a blind date?
- Ask for a raise?
- Give a speech?!

Each of these events usually triggers fear, inner anxiety, and self doubt. And each of these events is based on a host of **pre-existing** inner (hidden) decisions that command the body, mind and nervous system to react in a certain way.

The fact that these decisions were made as a small child -- or even in the womb or before -- doesn't matter. They are in place and control your actions, reactions, and outcomes. Goals and affirmations alone will not bring us out of it; <u>only the resolution of the source of the fear itself will solve this problem!</u>

Want to change that reaction?

Change the hidden decisions!

Hidden decisions actually govern your whole life. Consider the areas that are considered vital to your overall well-being that we most commonly try to "super-charge" by setting goals and repeating affirmations:

- Your health.
- Your intimate relationships.
- Your family relationships.
- Your wealth.

- Your ability to learn.
- Your ability to earn.
- Your ability to give.
- Your ability to accept.
- Your ability to love...

Each of these conditions or abilities is determined by the *quality of the decisions behind them*. If you feel weak inside, your outcomes will be restricted, and most certainly be weak. Alternately, if you can change the decision of the inner weakness to one of strength, your outcome will strengthen as well.

To change these hidden decisions, however, you need a way to

1. **Find out** if they are poisonous to your success.
2. **Get access** to them,
3. **Change** them quickly and easily and
4. **Integrate** them into your everyday reality.

Once access is gained, the whole world of hidden decisions becomes available without resorting to mind tricks, ineffective goal-setting programs, self-hypnosis, and years of affirmations that may or may not work by themselves.

Why Most Success Courses Don't Work

Let's face it, in addition to *Think and Grow Rich* there have been hundreds – nay, thousands - of books, tapes, programs and seminars on how to find success, wealth, and happiness from the same

The Logical Soul®

number of very successful entrepreneurs, artists, scientists, athletes, and others who know how to be successful, <u>but don't necessarily know the best way to get you there.</u>

So you buy their books, take their seminars, listen to their tapes and use their programs. When they don't work, it is naturally YOUR fault that you failed. (Read their legal disclaimers to get the full scope of your responsibility.)

It's a win-win. They get to be right because they *obviously* showed you the right way to commit to your goals and succeed. You, on the other hand, get to be right because you <u>proved</u> once again to yourself *"This won't work for me."* Your "right-brain wholeness" has too firm a grasp on your fate – and has little reason to change.

Now, think about that for a minute. At any given moment you decide on a goal, you either believe

a) You can do it or

b) You *can't* do it.

The body will instantly decide if (a) you can do this or (b) leave it alone, you can't do it, you're not going to do it... or *some other reason* that may be hidden from your conscious mind.

So when you set your goals,

- Wouldn't it be nice to have your **left** AND **right brain** on board?

- Wouldn't it be nice to have the **body** on board?

- Wouldn't it be nice to have the **emotions** on board?

- Wouldn't it be nice to have **intuition** come into play *effortlessly,* and

- Wouldn't it be nice if your **ancestors:** the memory of family, friends, and everything that's ever happened in your life supported you whenever you make a decision?

You can do this. All it takes is a few minutes, a few simple techniques, which I'll teach you in the following chapters, and then you'll be on your way.

The Logical Soul®

CHAPTER SIX

My Search for The Source

"There is more wisdom in your body than in your deepest philosophy."
- Friedrich Nietzsche

I failed many times in my life. In fact, I've failed many more times than I've succeeded.

I've been involved in business after business. I've had several relationships that failed. Two divorces. I've experienced many things in my life that just did not work out.

But I no longer see myself as a failure. I have been blessed – at a few critical times - with the ability to pull myself out of these tragedies, detox my mind, get back on my feet, and actually *realize* something about myself that I never knew before.

These realizations were a gift to me, so I pass them on to you. I want to share the idea that it's possible to achieve your goals <u>by getting congruent with</u>

them, NOT through wasted effort, repetition, suffering, or forced willpower.

The Wisdom of the Body

There is a *vast reservoir of intelligence, power and soul* deep within each of us. This power and this soul are very logical. Our right brains actually have both the ability AND motivation to make things happen at will.

Contrary to popular belief, emotions and logic are *not* opposed to one another. They're *not* mutually exclusive. But they must come to the same conclusions in order to work well together . . . to agree to the same life *decisions.* This is the essence of how to overcome self-sabotage.

I found in my years of work as a chiropractor, patients were not getting better. I used to agonize over this failure: "Why aren't they getting well? I'm doing all the right things. My technique is flawless. They're eating all the right things!" Everything on the surface seemed to be falling into place, but on some deep level the desired results were being blocked.

So what was I missing?

At the time I was practicing something called **applied kinesiology (AK).** For those of you not aware of this process, it is simply called "muscle testing," a simple built-in *biofeedback* mechanism that anyone can learn to use.

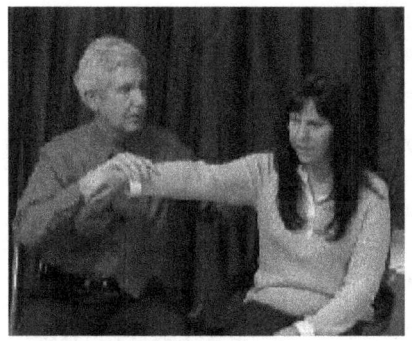
Try muscle testing with a partner, spouse or friend. Test any convenient muscle - say an arm muscle - by holding up their arm while using a few fingers to press on the arm after saying "Hold." If their arm tests strong (i.e., does not give under the pressure), that indicates a "yes" by the body. If the arm tests slightly weaker or rubbery (i.e., goes down), this may indicate a negative finding.

By testing this way, I was able to get feedback from the body that either this is a **yes** or **no** ("not yes").

Many doctors and therapists use this technique to get feedback from the mind/body to determine hidden incompatibility disorders, i.e.

(a) a certain substance is **good** for the body, or
(b) this substance is **not good** for the body.

I started using muscle testing for a different reason. I wanted to test for overall **congruence** of personal statements and affirmations.

After testing this way for several years, I became aware that the "yes" and "no" answers from the body begin to follow a predictable pattern. There was a kind of Morse code being transmitted here. It was as if our subconscious minds – mine and the patient's – were instantly revealing a sub-stratum of thoughts and decisions we had never known about before.

Excited, I started testing this method more and more on people. I also avoided attending other seminars and workshops while doing this research. I wanted to find out what the body, subconscious, or right brain was saying *to me directly* . . . *NOT* what someone else *told* me they were saying.

I learned that the body gathers up the sum total of *all inner decisions* and generates an outcome which may be either "yes" or "no." I also learned that the answers to these statements told of the immediate *outer condition* of the person as it pertained to the particular statement.

If, for example, you had problems with money, statements like "I choose to be a millionaire" would test false (weak). If you actually had the **capacity** within yourself to *become* a millionaire, however, that statement would be true (strong).

More trials and errors led me to find the secret to discovering the access to *any* inner (hidden) decision AND change them to be in alignment with current stated goals and affirmations.

> **Author's Note:** *I use A.K. for a particular limited purpose of affirmation feedback, and neither condone nor condemn its use for other purposes. Obviously, any technique so open to emotional interpretation should be considered experimental and not relied on solely as a regimen to diagnose and treat serious diseases or disorders. Consult with your physician or primary health practitioner before undertaking any such regimen.*

The Logical Soul®

The <u>Real</u> Law of Manifestation

<u>You must have a real sense of what you desire **inside** before it actually manifests in your world **outside.**</u> In fact, that's the way the mind works and world manifests: from above-down and inside-out!

If you ever have a thought about something like, "Hmm, I think I want some green tea and Thai food"?
First, there appears to be a feeling, i.e., the body says there's a hunger or thirst present. The feeling arises in the body that "I'm hungry." Then the memory kicks in, something like "I really *like* Thai food because it was *really tasty* last week!"

Once the thoughts and feelings converge inside, a desire arises: "I want Thai food." Then, you begin to make plans. You're feet begin to walk to the door, you grab your keys, you go to the car, you get into the car, you drive with your wife, boyfriend, girlfriend to the Thai restaurant; you sit, you order, the green tea and food comes, and you eat.

Then something happens: the **fulfillment** of that desire takes place. But really, what happened first? Was it the *thought* or was it the *impulse* that brought the thought about? The answer is - the impulse happened first.

The *impulse* arises and then it is followed by the thought. After the thought comes *action* . . . then *achievement* takes place, i.e., being at the Thai restaurant and ordering the food. Then the fulfillment of that desire: tasting the food.

So, if you want something to happen *outside,* the **Law of Manifestation** states that you must first have this impulse, this thought, this desire *inside.* Something arises within your consciousness that says "I want this," then the thought manifests itself as an outside ripple of actions and events. This means that

- Thoughts are not something that you **do.**
- Thoughts are things that you **have.**
- Thoughts *arise* from **deep within your consciousness.**

You Can Direct Your Destiny

Now, with the *Logical Soul®* you can find out *where* those impulses lie, *where* those thoughts actually come from. You can tap into that hidden reservoir of thought previously unavailable to you.

You will soon discover the **reasons** as to **why** certain thoughts, feelings and desires arise within you in the first place. You will also learn *how to change and redirect them when necessary!*

So long as the original reasons are there, <u>all you can do is have the original thought and desire</u>. And, consequently, you can only have the original (i.e., predestined) outcome.

If you want different outcomes, tap into that hidden reservoir of intelligence and desire. *Find out where the thought comes from.*

It's very simple to do. Using the feedback techniques I will cover in this book -- and the method of questioning I will share with you -- you'll be able to tap into these things quickly, within minutes.

You'll be able to <u>at last</u> **change decisions on a very deep level** and create what you want *inside* so that very soon you'll be able to manifest your goals *outside.*

CHAPTER SEVEN

The Discovery of Access

"One does not discover new lands without consenting to lose sight of the shore for a very long time."
- André Gide

Cathy's Wake Up Call

Access was not something I set out to discover. The year was 1992, and one day it just happened.

I was in a meeting with Cathy (not her real name), a friend of mine who expressed an interest in going into business with me as corporate consultants. She was experienced in this type of business, and I felt honored to be asked to visit her home to discuss the possibilities.

I had a few reservations, however. One was the feeling that we might be glossing over some difficulties. I felt there was some kind of disconnect between our goals of making money in consulting, and actually seeing that money show up. I thought it would be a good idea to muscle test each other to find out if we had the **inner resolve** to undertake this joint venture successfully.

It turns out we didn't. While I don't remember my responses, I do remember Cathy's. There was something in her energy field or body that blocked her from making the type of business commitment necessary for our success.

I had elicited this type of feedback many times before as a chiropractor, i.e., I used muscle testing or AK to test the body's attraction or aversion to certain substances or ideas. This part of the procedure was routine for me.

What *WAS* new was the way in which I chose to resolve the problem. In the past, I would use someone else's idea of "integration points" on the body – similar to acupuncture points – to find and "fix" the problem. I also knew how to run meridians, move energy around in the body, and generally make myself feel better that I accomplished something. I had to admit in all honesty, however, that these exercises seldom brought about long-term results.

There are lots of New Age rituals designed to supposedly raise consciousness and heal the body-mind of all deep impressions. A touch here. A tap there. Running some meridian lines over here; then "sealing the chakras" at the end with the aid of "spiritual guides and masters." These healing systems are usually all based on some theory by a doctor or practitioner, and have very official names with words in them like "technology" "bio-energetic" and "synchronous."

I was willing to try them all, but knew their effects didn't last long. Very few methods – chiropractic or new age - actually made any real difference over time. While I could see some definite short-term benefits, it was all so subjective. In fact, I found that doing ANYTHING to the body, so long as it sounded official, had a similar effect.

I felt I was giving mostly *placebos:* harmless, but not how I wanted to spend my time. There had to be another way to bring about *real* changes in people's mindsets, behavior and overall well-being.

I decided to try something different with Cathy, but I didn't really know what. All I had was the *intent* to invite a transformation that was noticeably real and measurable.

I didn't even know how to proceed, other than to use muscle testing and ask the body questions . . . that is until I hit **"The Wall,"** that invisible barrier that prevented further exploration into the hidden realms of the mind and subconscious.

(The Wall also guards our deeply *hidden decisions* - our source of inner power and creative intelligence. You will find out more about this in Chapter 21.)

The reason I called it *The Wall* was because it appeared to be a barrier that expressed itself through more symptoms of *confusion* and *dissonance.* In other words, the muscle testing might produce both "yes" and "no" answers to the same statement or question, the person might go blank, or he or she might exhibit increased nervousness, anger, or loss of focus.

Not quite knowing what I was doing with Cathy, I somehow discovered a way *beyond* the Wall. The reason I knew this was because she suddenly reported feeling excruciating pain, anxiety, and the sensation that she was going to die!

I didn't know what to do. I tried to talk her down again, tapped on a few points, then let her go. This apparently didn't solve the problem, however, because her boyfriend called me later demanding that I *"fix her or else..."*

I gladly complied and spent another day with Cathy, working, talking, testing, and experimenting with various approaches. Eventually I was able to get her to a point of stability, and to some degree of happiness. After a while she even became *enthusiastic* about this new technique I had discovered, but more on this later.

With the discovery of ACCESS, I found I could unlock the explosive power of the body and mind at will. I later put in some safety measures and distilled the whole *Logical Soul®* process into a simple technique that anyone can use to remove the barriers to effectiveness in action, and to achieve rapid personal transformation.

****

To understand this thing called *Access* let's first take a look at how the mind and body works . . .

The Logical Soul®

Our Conscious Handicap

Discounting bodily functions (which may number in the billions), your brain *alone* has the raw power to processes *between* **1 trillion and 100 trillion operations per second!!** [15] Some studies show this figure as high as 100 *quadrillion!)* Sensory nerves feed countless packets of stimuli to the brain each nano-second pertaining to light, sound, touch, smell, and taste.

The vast majority of these stimuli are filtered out, i.e., they never reach the conscious mind. Why? Because *we can't* process *that much stimuli*, much less use *it!*

Your *conscious* mind, by contrast, can process only *4 to 7 bits of data* at any given time (see *Appendix D)*. In one way this is a tremendous disadvantage since 99.9999999% of sensory input simply never reaches the "control tower" of your cerebrum. Gone! Wiped out!

All this extra unprocessed stimuli gets dumped into the body somewhere, or vibrated off into our surroundings . . . including the brains and nervous systems of other people. Without this feedback, we cannot possibly know what is happening to us consciously all the time.

When was the last time, for example, you *consciously* digested your lunch? Or made your heart beat? Didn't happen, right?

On the other hand, without all that stimuli to clog up our minds, we can think clearer and pull memory up as needed from our inner files. While the mind may not remember a lot of "stuff," the body certainly does.

Mesmerizing Facts

Accessing this so-called "body memory," however, has been a trick of smoke and mirrors ever since the Austrian healer **Franz Anton Mesmer** tantalized the French Royal Court of Louis XVI in the mid-18th Century with his flair for what he called "animal magnetism." Since then, the art and science of hypnosis has been developed as a way to tap into the mind-body's amazing capacity for suggestion on a deep level.

While **hypnosis** may allow us to access our subconscious mind in order to plant suggestions, it does **not** seem to allow us to *access and change fundamental hidden decisions* – a sort of "de-hypnotizing" process for pre-verbal programming, a vital step in changing our lives. While we may become aware of the abuse our uncle laid on us at age three, for example, we may not know the mechanism needed to change the unconscious [hidden] decision that still governs and affects our adult life.

Even if we do somehow make the right hypnotic suggestion that changes one or two key decisions, *hypnotic suggestion is based on* **conscious choices** by either the practitioner or the subject. Changes made consciously FOR our subconscious mind carry with it the risk that the subconscious will rebel and either kick out the suggestion or negatively affect other areas of our life.

Also, hypnosis does not always provide *Access* to the hidden recesses of our minds that have sealed themselves off from ANY intrusion by force or trickery. While we might be able to fool ourselves into thinking something happened, with proper testing we find nothing has changed. Such is the power of our original intent!

The body's "inner wisdom" is available, however, for all those who know how to tap into it. All you need is to be able to:

a) Access and change hidden decisions,
b) Bring this wisdom to the surface, and
c) Consciously integrate success into your life.

You need the process I call the *Logical Soul®*.

The Meaning of Soul "Logic"

The words "soul" and "logic" uttered together appear strange. We are not used to hearing them in the same sentence. Yet these words describe the only process that actually works, i.e., using an actual technique to access and change something formerly assigned to the region of the soul.

My journey into the soul was not consciously undertaken since I didn't know what to do or where to go! The soul itself seeks to make its presence known to my conscious mind and continues to lead me into this realm of mystery and revelation.

Critical decisions I made about things like choice of being, associations, food, when and where to sleep, who to have sex with, the type of work I do, and how to bring about transformation in my life - all played a part. My life is like that of others in many ways, but *unlike* others in the sequence and order of decisions that are *unique only to me.*

My life has been a vehicle that has so far led me to one major conclusion: that **the Soul has an inherent logic in it.** It breathes both life AND structure; and for that I am grateful.

And so is Cathy.

CHAPTER EIGHT

Cartoons and Gurus: A Seeker's Guide to Hidden Decisions

"Don't take life too seriously. You'll never get out alive."
- Bugs Bunny

My life has been the canvas on which a series of major turning points have been embroidered. Here are a few more of the ones that led to my own hidden decisions:

Looney Tunes Strikes Again

I don't know if it was because I had my "third eye" smacked open or what. Until I was eleven years old, however, I believed that everyone – including myself – were all cartoon characters.

This was understandable, in part, since my Saturday morning and after-school world largely consisted of *Bugs Bunny, Yosemite Sam, Donald Duck, Peter Pan,*

Superman, and other characters invited into my life through TV and comic books.

The good news was that life was *fiercely fun,* and my grades didn't seem to be affected except to draw complaints from my teachers who reported I "day-dreamed too much." I still made honor roll every year, however, and was usually popular with classmates.

The bad news was that I did things that alarmed my parents and elders on a regular basis. Because I saw life as usually non-threatening, things like heights, strangers, big dogs, and sharp objects rarely made me pause to consider the consequences. I considered my body as part of the playground I was given to play in, that's all.

One day my friend David shot out my tooth with a BB gun. I picked up the dislodged canine and ran home yelling to my Mom something about getting rich that night from the Tooth Fairy! Apparently she didn't find this amusing since my Dad later had a long talk with me about the importance of NOT getting shot in the head with guns.

The other problem with living in a cartoon world was that I believed that living things never died or even got hurt. I learned the error of my thinking one day when David and I spent the afternoon playing with our new kittens – occasionally submerging them in a large bucket of water. The resulting whipping I got from my Dad made me realize that animals have feelings too.

I respected animals from that day onward. In fact, I could not kill *any* of them for *any* reason. My Dad probably realized he had created a monster when I started throwing fish back, became a vegetarian, avoided stepping on ants, and screamed to save roaches from the exterminator.

I had made a decision: Never harm an animal or you get a whipping.

Seal It with a Kiss

While animals became real, this honor didn't extend to humans for a long time. To me they were still *Yosemite Sam, Olive Oyl, Tinker Bell, Foghorn Leghorn,* and *Huckleberry Hound.* Fun characters all.

Other kids would get mad; I'd laugh. They would hit me; I'd laugh. They would cry; I'd laugh. Even adults were part of this cartoon world: *Mr. Green Jeans, Mr. Wilson, Ward Cleaver, George Jetson,* and *Barney Rubble* would try to hide their "true identity" from me, but I knew who they *really* were!

I also found out such rampant fun can be dangerous. One afternoon after school I chased a male friend around an empty classroom trying to kiss him. I wasn't gay – he was just such a spitting image of *Deputy Dawg* I couldn't resist! Besides, the fact that he ran from me made the whole thing (to me anyway) hilarious.

I soon discovered the penalty for invading someone's space. My friend reported me to the Principal and I received a severe tongue lashing. When questioned about my sexual orientation, I didn't know what to say since I had no idea about sex at that age (11). I was forced to apologize to the student and teachers, and for the rest of my school years I simply "served time," i.e., shut down my feelings and buried my enthusiasm.

Lesson learned.

Since this also happened the same year that my great-grandmother and John F. Kennedy died, my world suddenly became very real. To survive in this new world without cartoons, I sought protection using the best way I knew, i.e., crawling into an emotional hole and hiding until graduation.

The world was suddenly scary. Despite earlier flashes of brilliance, I soon ranked near the middle of my small graduating class. I was able to survive with a couple of close friends, a huge collection of Marvel comics, and visions of super powers eventually being bestowed upon me to save the world.

I became what my elders considered to be an "underachiever." My cartoon world still persisted, but the funny characters were replaced by more serious ones: Superman, Spider Man, and others with secret identities.

By the middle of sixth grade I had made both an observation and a **decision:** Hey, these crazy folks out there are *real!* And it's freaking *dangerous* to let them know who I *really* am and what I *really* feel!

I Feel the Earth Move

My super powers arrived, but not the way I expected.

By the time I was age 13, rampant hormones coupled with self-isolation created a real need for an outlet. I found mine through *astronomy*.

Armed with a new telescope I got for Christmas and the extra time I gained from not being at all social, I spent every night for over a year under the stars – plotting the path of the moon and planets, charting the Milky Way constellations, observing the orbiting moons of Jupiter, and searching for far-off star clusters and nebulae.

One gorgeous moonless night I had the urge to just cap the telescope and lie there in my backyard. As I gazed into the abyss I let my mind go and my body relax. I had no thoughts, no agenda, and no need for anything. It was a rare moment of absolute peace.

Then out of nowhere, that peace transformed itself into a blinding flash of knowingness. Awareness suddenly shifted from body and mind to the sudden realization that I WAS the earth, the stars and the empty space.

I WAS the dew on my face . . . and the grass beneath the body. The "I" ebbed and flowed, until there was a realization that I WAS no longer there! There was a "seeing" into the void that contains all things – earth, heaven and everything in between. This place had both the greatest bliss *and* strongest fear I could imagine...

I had NO words to describe what was happening to me. In fact, I was no longer "me."

This freaked me out . . . and with the thought came release. Just as suddenly as it appeared, the vision of One-ness left. I found myself "back" with no clue as to what had happened. I was simply aware, for the first time, that life surged through this body and that "I" was no longer the owner. I calmly grabbed the telescope and made my way inside.

Although I never lost this feeling, forgetfulness gradually allowed the memory of that night to be all but lost - until meditation reawakened it years later.

For the next several years I felt torn between the need to be alone in this silence, and the pull of my VERY LOUD family and school. I tried my best to stay isolated from others, and apparently came across to others as stuck up and aloof. Consequently, I suffered much bullying and indignities as a teenager, but figured that was the price I had to pay for keeping my "secret identity" safe. As a result, I resigned myself to being banished from any form of social life.

Decision Made: I'm really different. No one understands me, so I can never talk about it!

That Guru Thing

Once free of high school and into college (where few people knew me) I went crazy with the usual mix of sex, drugs and rock and roll. Nothing was too extreme during those times and my parents worried endlessly.

It was meditation that saved my life. After a particularly insightful LSD experience I made a decision: give my life to Jesus, or start doing *Transcendental Meditation^{tm}*. Since the Jesus commune was closed that day, I chose TM.

I moved back home with my relieved parents and started cleansing both body and mind. The changes were soon noticeable. I sweated out gallons of stress and started feeling better than ever before. I felt alive, healthy. I also hung out with local TM teachers who convinced me to go to California to be

The Logical Soul®

with Maharishi Mahesh Yogi. Excited about the prospect, I signed up.

Meditation with the Maharishi had such a calming effect on my mind and body I worked to save money to eventually travel to Switzerland and France, to a TM teacher training course in 1973. Those years were amongst my happiest. Although I went back to college and did other things, I *really* enjoyed teaching TM. I guess I finally felt like I was part of something universal – bringing back that *expansive* feeling again.

It also lured me into thinking that the whole world would start meditating soon. They didn't of course, and my success with teaching ended with a thud around 1976.

It took me another 24 years, two failed marriages, and nineteen failed jobs or ventures before I woke up and realized I was suffering from what I lovingly call **"Post-Guru Syndrome,"** a condition that strikes without warning and lasts for decades. Because teaching TM was such an expansive gig, nothing else came close. It became like an endorphin addiction, and withdrawal from it proved traumatic to my other goals and aspirations which, by comparison, appeared to be mundane.

The **symptoms of PGS** include: avoidance of all stress, having strict rules about diet and routine, a general acceptance of everything the Guru says and does, smiling a lot, measuring time as intervals between meditation or courses, inability to completely share with outsiders, and classifying everything as either "gross" or "refined," and avoiding all things gross and hanging out with the refined. After quitting the guru, one can also feel useless, ill-fitted for society, strangely despondent, and most often detached.

The biggest problem with PGS victims is that they don't know they are victims. I didn't. I actually thought I was on the verge of enlightenment - a blessed member of an elite group of "Governors of the Age of Enlightenment" carrying on the tradition of Masters, "governing the trends of time" and changing world events by mere intent. This was really cool.

Detached? No problem – the world was an illusion anyway. So long as I was fed and had a place to sleep and meditate, the world was great!

I first suspected I had a problem when I volunteered to be on a local TV talk show to bring Maharishi's message to the world – that people were *flying*. While some long-term practitioners were actually lifting off the ground and bouncing on mattresses scattered around the floor, Maharishi's proclaimed that his "Flying Siddhis" would transform the world in a few short years.

Although *I* had not yet experienced the Siddhis – and was not fully aware of Maharishi's unbounded capacity to exaggerate - I was convinced I should do as Maharishi requested and "tell all the people" . . .

"That's fantastic. Have you flown yourself?" asked the interviewer.

"Well, no, but..."

"Have you *seen* anyone flying?" he asked again with raised eyebrow.

"No."

"Thank you for coming on the show."

Oops.

Publicly humiliated, I stopped teaching TM and "Post Guru Syndrome" set in big time. Although I later hopped around on mattresses myself, somehow the thrill was gone.

Circumstances had guided me to **the major decision of my adult life:** Don't get too excited about stuff because life is empty and meaningless (a reinforcement of the first thing I learned as a child: "Life hurts when you're rambunctious").

CHAPTER NINE

The Discovery of Soul Logic

*"He's a real nowhere man,
Sitting in his nowhere land
Making all his nowhere plans
for nobody."*
- Lennon-McCartney

Emotional Surgery

The 1980's were kind of a blur to me. I attended and graduated from Chiropractic College, got my license in Georgia, got divorced from my first wife, struggled in practice, and married my second wife.

Oh, and the midst of all of this I attracted an older woman into my life.

Drenda was intense, older than me by eight years . . . and most likely bi-polar. She was also my designated "emotional surgeon." Before Drenda arrived my life was nice, neat and orderly, full of charts, processes, and a steady routine: eat, sleep, meditate, and work. After she arrived, my life became pure chaos.

Drenda latched onto me and took me on the ride of my life: wild parties, camping trips, nudist colony visits, and high-speed chases in low-speed neighborhoods. I couldn't even get away from her and hated myself for it, but somehow felt really special because of her intense attachment to me.

This illusion of being special came crashing down around me when she started getting violent, making threats of suicide and bought a gun. She then used this tactic to keep me from leaving her. And it worked; for months anyway.

When I finally got up the nerve to escape and hide, she blew her brains out. I was devastated; it took years for me to recover.

My new-found freedom was a mixed blessing. I still had a hole in my heart and looked to positive thinking seminars to help me fill it. I met new friends and married my second wife Carol, someone I considered emotionally "safe." I also started getting migraine headaches, and experienced periodic depression and more failed jobs and businesses.

The new inner decisions in my life: Life is *not* as it seems, and can be dangerous! Take control and stay positive – the negative can kill you!

Adventure in Sri Lanka

I started having migraine headaches after Drenda's death that often got really intense. In an effort to alleviate the pain, I got regular chiropractic adjustments (of course), but also started studying Chinese medicine.

Acupuncture study was an odd choice for me, however, since I hated needles. Ever since I was a little tyke confined to the hospital for repeated tests and treatments, I hated getting shots. It was months before I finally allowed someone to treat a liver point in my foot for the migraines.

I fainted.

When I awoke a few minutes later, the pain in my head had subsided, but I had another pain in my foot – a burning pain that got worse as time went on.

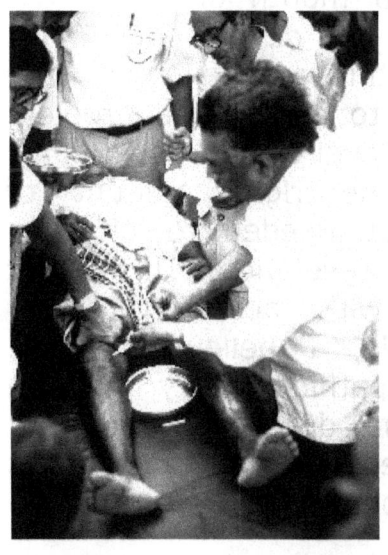

"Take it out!" The acupuncturist complied, and the pain went away. (I never fainted from needles after that, but to this day I still hesitate before allowing myself to be stuck.)

Intrigued, I read every book I could find on the subject, and talked over things with my wife. We soon made a decision to leave my practice and travel to the Buddhist country of **Sri Lanka** (formerly Ceylon) to study acupuncture with the international expert and author on the subject, **Dr. Anton Jayasuriya,** at Kalibuwila Hospital, outside Colombo. The year was 1987.

The Logical Soul®

This journey transformed my life – physically, mentally, emotionally and spiritually. I even wrote a novel about it in 1996 based on true events called *The Remedies of Pachili* (available soon). This book tells of a mystical journey to the island, spiritual awakening and contact with the island's ancient past.

Many events that took place in the novel were based on true stories. One such episode happened in the hospital and changed my perception about what is physically possible. It had to do with a young boy with *rickets* – a bone-softening disease said to be caused by a lack of *vitamin D.*

After a month or so at the clinic I had developed a knack for intuitive healing – the ability to diagnose a problem at the level of cause and apply only the right amount of stimulus needed to affect a cure or resolution. This meant that, with acupuncture for example, I believed in the homeopathic theory of the "minimal dose," i.e., applying a remedy only to those points which would change the body's energy, and no more.

While many doctors and practitioners applied needles for relief of symptoms, my training as a chiropractor led me to automatically look for the innate *cause* instead. I trusted this ability and it seldom failed me. Even so, I was unprepared for what happened one hot August morning.

That day a woman brought in her young son of about 10 years old to see what I could do for his *rickets.* My initial thought was to just provide some homeopathic relief and suggest she give him some vitamins to alleviate his condition. My intuition, however, was strongly telling me to simply hold my fingers on some points on his back and legs. This I did, after having him lie face down on my chiropractic table.

Unexpectedly, and despite the fact I used only my fingers and no needles, the boy began to cry and thrash about so much that I asked for help to hold him down. Two men complied while I continued to hold the same points.

By now, also, the points were heating up to the point of burning my fingertips. I held on in spite of the pain. I could sense that something major was happening here and didn't want to cut it short.

Thirty minutes after beginning what turned out to be a very intense session, the pain decreased and the boy fell asleep. When he later got off the table I observed that, as he walked away, his legs were straight with no limp!

This sight was so unexpected, I rationalized that maybe his legs were not so crooked before. His mother set me straight when she came and bowed down at my feet the next day. Feeling uncomfortable, I quickly asked her to rise. When I saw the tears in her eyes, however, my heart expanded and my mind temporarily ceased all its chatter.

I never forgot that incident, and came to appreciate why the ancient name for the island was **Serendib,** the root of the word *Serendipity* which was coined by an 18th century English writer and means *"the faculty of making happy and unexpected discoveries by accident."* [15]

Later in 1992, the incident with Cathy (see Chapter 7) revealed a new tool – **Access** – and it became apparent there was a plan for my life. While it was consciously unexpected, something was obviously at play here with an intelligence all its own. Call it Divine power, God, or Spirit, *something* was playing with me.

My new inner decision was best expressed by Hamlet: *"There are more things in heaven and earth, Horatio, than are dreamt of in your philosophy."*

Wandering in the Wilderness

Between the years 1992 and 2008, I worked with patients and friends using my new-found technique I now call the *Logical Soul®*. The fact is, however, I had no idea what I had, and was unable to communicate this procedure very well. Cathy, my wife Brigitte (Soma), and another mutual friend, however, thought it was great and created a small mastermind group to "work on their stuff" over a period of several years.

Apparently there were no rules. Their *stuff* was endless and their sessions became more and more esoteric and New-Age. After a few months of hanging out with them, I finally decided it didn't feel right and got involved in other things. The women appeared to derive benefit from these sessions, however, and I was happy for them to continue.

I still had some burdens to bear: tangles with the IRS, depression, deep-seated anger, lack of mental and emotional clarity, and finally some relief. Throughout it all, Soma kept urging me to *"write your book!"* At the time, however, I felt so depressed and victimized that the idea of telling people about how much it helped me seemed a bit ludicrous.

I got involved with real estate for ten years and continued working on myself using the *Logical Soul®*. Eventually I was able to sell our little island vacation property and earn a tidy profit that all went towards paying off the mountain of debt. My relief was palpable.

Regardless of how much I enjoyed real estate and other projects, however, I never really felt passionate about them. Working on various projects simply gave me an excuse to postpone writing this book on the *Logical Soul®* - what Soma describes as my "real work."

The wake-up call came in Macon, Georgia in mid-2008 during lunch with friends. It <u>finally</u> sunk in that **many others** wanted this book to come out . . . and I'd been putting it off for *sixteen years!* So I started writing again.

Suddenly, it felt right.

CHAPTER TEN

How to Assess Your Inner Dialogue and Goal-to-Action Conflicts

*"We have been sitting idly by most of our lives
While we have let George run the show
in any hit-or-miss way he might choose."*
- Max Freedom Long,
discussing the role of his
subconscious mind (George).

Why Can't We All Just Get Along . . .

Inner dialogue – or **"self talk"** – is the constant chatter that goes on behind closed minds. Does *your* inner chatter support your goals and aspirations? Or does it – like most mind noise - make you feel overwhelmed, under prepared, stupid,

85

The Logical Soul®

weak, or heading towards failure? Only *you* can determine what it is and how to stop or change it.

But *how*?

How do you properly assess such inner dialogue to determine whether or not this noise contains seeds of success or failure, i.e., **goal-to-action conflicts?**

Since self talk or inner dialogue is constantly going on, the question is, does this dialogue support your goals, support your affirmations and what you want to do with your life? Does it allow you to be fulfilled?

Or is your self-talk delivering monologues like *"I can't do that," "I shouldn't do that"* or *"I'm really bad if I do that"*?

Most of us, while we are aware of such inner talk, don't really know how to turn it off. We try to do so by using various means like meditation to let go of the self talk, or by creating affirmations, writing them over and over and over again.

Affirmations are great. The only problem is, our inner self-talk is so strong and firmly anchored in, *it would take us full time saying and writing down affirmations and goals just to make a dent in our consciousness!*

The Great Ones would still have you do this. Why? Because it worked for them! They will tell you to make notes of everything you say to yourself; write it down. Write down the conversations you have with yourself, then write down your goals and repeat them. Over and over, until it happens. Or *shout* them out as part of a group in a pep-rally-rah-rah setting.

These are all great exercises, but 96% or more of the human race won't do them or play all out. Most are just going through the motions. *It takes a lot of time or effort to do,* and few people will devote that amount of time or that much effort, *even if it means their lives will change dramatically.*

The good news is that you don't HAVE to practice these repetitious or laborious tasks. You can actually *test your body at any given time* for any decision you make to find out if your self talk supports your goals. If it does, great! Nothing to do except smile and go on your way!

If the self-talk shoots down your goals, don't despair. You can also test your body to find the hidden decisions that give rise to the negative self-talk. This is because *your self talk essentially is your body speaking* - your body, your nervous system, your memory, your intuition and emotions.

All hidden decisions speak through your body. Your body becomes like the nexus point, i.e., the point at which the rubber meets the road (so to speak) with your intentions and your goals.

So if your body is saying, *"I can't do this,"* then you must pretty much believe that that's what is true, i.e., you can't do this. You've heard the expression that *"if you think you can, you can and if you think you can't?"* That's true also.

That's the way the body is. The body will give you feedback, so writing stuff down over and over again to try to counter-balance that negative self talk is a waste of time and not necessary.

In this book you will learn a technique that you can use to . . .

- discover your inner dialogue and
- discover whether or not your body is saying *Yes* or *No* to any particular statement or affirmation you make.

Would you like to learn how to do that? It's very simple and it takes just a few minutes. Here's how to get started . . .

Find out what the body is saying.
The body has its own language, and this language is logical. The *Logical Soul®* means that logic is *inherent* in the body and soul.

> (**Note**: I use the term "soul" to summarize all that which goes on inside of us – our bodies, our mind, our emotions, our memory, our intuition - all of these are different levels of the soul. So the term "Soul" is all inclusive as far as this book is concerned.)

To test the logic inherent in the soul (and not just in our mind) we must have proper procedures for **bio-feedback.** It's very simple - not all scientifically accurate - but accurate enough to give us feedback that we need, in order to make an honest assessment at any given moment.

The technical or scientific name for this feedback is *Applied Kinesiology*. The less-fancy name is *muscle testing*.

How to Muscle Test

Muscle testing is done very simply by using a spouse or significant other, maybe a friend or family member to help you. Just have this person sit next to you in order to test their arm, or have them test your arm. Have the person hold out his or her arm and use *about two to three pounds of pressure* to just press on that arm to see whether or not it is strong.

- **If the arm is strong (stays up),** this indicates a "yes" answer to an affirmation or statement.

- **If the arm is weak or rubbery (goes down),** this indicates a "no" (or "not yes") answer to an affirmation or statement.

This is a powerful way of testing Affirmations. The reason is because at any given moment, our conscious minds can only hold so much information, compared to the **trillions** of bits of data that zip around our neural circuits each second.

If you want to remember a phone number for example, you have to say it over and over in your head walking from one end of the house to the other. You might repeat "1, 2, 3, 4, 5, 6, 7. . . 1, 2,

3, 4, 5. . ." over and over to yourself. If somebody asks you a question, suddenly all is forgotten. Why? It's too much for the conscious mind to handle, and you lose your train of thought.

The body on the other hand can process several **trillion** bits of information at any given time. It gathers all that information up and gives you a "yes" (based on the information it knows to be true) or a "no."

This is a tremendously valuable tool that you can use at any given moment to find out

    a) where you are heading and
    b) how you are going to get there.

How to Self-Test

Another way of muscle testing the body i.e., finding out if the body is saying yes or no *without* a partner is to use **self testing.**

There are various means of self testing, but none are as accurate as using a partner, quite frankly. However, the self-testing methods I will teach you are very good in a pinch, and much better than nothing.

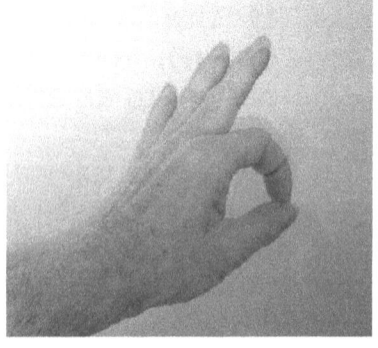

The method I like to use most is the one where you take your **thumb and index finger** and create like an "OK" sign. If you are right-handed, create the

The Logical Soul®

sign with your left hand (see photo). If left-handed, use the right hand.

Next, stick the index finger of the other hand through the loop and try to **break that loop** by briskly hitting the side of the index finger against the point of contact between the loop made by your other thumb and index finger. Do this several times to get a feel for this action.

Once you feel ready, formulate a positive statement such as *"My name is* (state your name).*"* Then test. If you said your name correctly, the loop should hold.

For example, if I do this while saying *"My name is Michael,"* the loop will remain strong and not allow my opposite-hand finger to break through, indicating a "strong" or "yes." If I say *"My name is Sally,"* it should break the loop and I will get what is called a "negative finding" or a "No."

Do this until you consistently get a "yes" or "no" based on your known statements such as *"I have a million dollars in the bank"* (no) or *"I raise llamas in my backyard"* (this will probably test weak). Once we get reliable readings on **known** positive and negative statements, we can proceed further and test for **unknown** positive or negative statements.

Here is the summary:
Loop holds = Strong = *Yes finding* = True statement
Loop gives way = Weak = *No finding* = False or "not true"

Exceptions. If for some reason you *don't* seem to be able to get any clear-cut answers (yes or no), you may have an issue with trusting your instincts or intuition, and may need to get a partner or practitioner to do the testing for you. That is a more powerful approach anyway.

Also, this technique will usually not work if you are a committed left-brainer or on heavy medication. It seldom works for habitual liars, sociopaths, and if you are drunk or stoned; those with deep-seated personality disorders, addictive or bi-polar disorders.

> **NOTE:** *If you have been diagnosed as bi-polar, do a Google search for Ken Jensen to learn his drug-free way out of this affliction. He can also refer you to the right sources for help if needed.*

The above rare exceptions, however, should not stop you from trying it out. Use this simple self-help technique to test statements on different facets of your life. Let's use the example of money because that seems to be an issue that plagues a lot of people these days.

Testing for Money Issues

To test for money, there are **seven elements** involved, which I cover in more depth in my 2011 book *The Money Matrix Method*™:

1. how much am I <u>worth</u>,
2. how much can I <u>easily earn</u>,
3. how much can I <u>accept</u>, and
4. how much am I willing to <u>Act on</u>?
5. Presence of Father
6. Presence of Mother, and
7. Presence of Ancestors.

Let's just make a statement, i.e., "*I'm worth at least a million dollars*" and show you are weak on that. This means that your self-worth is **not** yet a million dollars. If you show strong on that statement, great! Then test for increasing amounts until you show weak.

If you show strong on *every* amount and *every* statement you test for, you're either

- a) very rich and have NO money issues,
- b) not testing correctly (go back and practice testing with known statements), or
- c) you have an ability to lie to yourself at a very deep level.

Once you determine there is a limit to your earning capacity, worth or ability to accept, you have gone half the distance to solving the problem. In later chapters, I'll go over how to get access to and resolve these issues.

The Inner Decision-Maker

During the first year after I discovered **access** and the whole Logical Soul® process, I started piecing together the answers I was getting from patients and others. I learned there was a *real intelligence* at work, and a power that I had never been privy to before.

I called this inner power "*The One Who Makes Things Happen.*" I simply did not know what else to name it.

Then one day in 1993 as I walked down my hallway, a book fell from the hallway shelf and opened on the floor. Picking it up, I noticed it was a hard-back book that a friend had given me about ten years earlier entitled *The Secret Science at Work* by Max Freedom Long.

It was an old book, published in the early 1950's, and was based on the work of Max Long who spent decades exploring Hawaii to find clues about the ancient shamans who performed such miracles as walking on fire and healing the sick. Long found that words used by the **Huna and Kahuna shamans** gave vital clues and procedures about how these were done.

> (**NOTE:** In 1953, fire walking was considered a "miracle." Today it is not only accepted as possible, but is fairly commonplace in self-help circles, thanks to the pioneering work of Anthony Robbins.)

Long discovered that the *Kahunas* saw the so-called "individual" as **three selves** - distinct and unique – who were bound together and could either work together, or fight each other. They each had their own powers and sphere of control, and miracles occurred when they were in harmony. This knowledge, in fact, pre-dated Freud by thousands of years.

I was floored. Out of the blue came this book - that I had overlooked for ten years – arriving at the exact time I needed an answer to one burning question: *who or what was this internal personality that guided us?* I spent the next two weeks reading this book over and over, making notes, and ordering other books by Long and other experts on *Kahuna* lore.

The scope of *Huna* knowledge was more than sufficient to describe - in detail – what I had discovered independently with the *Logical Soul®*. I kept reading, hoping to add to my knowledge and bring out more and more methods of strengthening inner congruence and personal power.

Similar Shamanic legends are evident in Sri Lanka. The power of the original spirit people – the *yaksas* and *nagas* – is kept alive through "devil dancing," fire walking, and *yaka* masks in Sinhalese culture.

Apparently it is also kept alive in the wondrous healings that I witnessed taking place in the clinic.

CHAPTER ELEVEN

The Three Selves

"Alright men, fire at will!" - Moe
"Which one is Will?" - Curley
(the Three Stooges)

If you already have the *Seeds of Success*, you are truly blessed. Congratulations! You can skip this chapter unless you just like reading stories.

For the rest of us, knowing about the three selves is crucial. Why? Because this knowledge will unlock the secret to getting **congruent** – both inside and out – so that you can attract whatever you want into your life. Without congruence, our *Seed of Failure* will persist and bear more fruit.

> **Disclaimer:** The material presented in this and other chapters is a practical model, or paradigm, you can use to understand your inner motivation. It is not to be taken as "the Truth," or as a way to diagnose or treat disease. As always, consult your physician first.

The Search for Kahuna Magic

Max Freedom Long discovered these "selves" during his search for the stories about how the **Kahunas** – or original Hawaiian shamans – performed their miracles. In his study of the ancient Polynesian language, he came across words that told these stories about how the shamans could walk on burning hot lava, heal the sick, and control inner bodily functions.

Many of these so-called miracles have today become commonplace. In the 1980's, **Tony Robbins** became one of the first few westerners to teach fire walking and demonstrate other aspects of our subconscious power to large numbers of people. Today, we have simply to turn on the *Discovery Channel* to catch the latest exploits of another miracle-worker or urban shaman.

The underlying principles of these miracles have not changed. To be congruent and powerful, you must have a laser-like focus and connection between the conscious and subconscious minds. These aspects - what we consider as "mind" in the west – have a much deeper and richer meaning in much of Asia, and in the Hawaiian **Huna,** or "secret."

Max Freedom Long was the re-discoverer of the Huna in the 1930's and author of many books on the subject. He based much of his research on the 1865 edition of "A Dictionary of the Hawaiian Language" by Lorrin Andrews, where the word "Huna" means:

> *"To hide or conceal; to keep from the sight or knowledge of another. To conceal, as knowledge or wisdom. That which is concealed*

(in conversation or writing this definition is expressed as 'ka huna.')" [16]

The "Ka-Hunas" (*Kahunas*) kept this secret in order to preserve the knowledge of real power from being diluted or destroyed by western explorers and missionaries. Long was able to re-construct much of this knowledge by studying the language of the ancient Polynesians, and deciphering the hidden meanings.

Long found, for example, words in the native language that described in detail the **"three selves"** and other phenomenon he described as the "three kinds of vital force" and even "complexes" as we know them in modern psychology. According to Long, the *Kahunas* had a name for each of these three selves:

- **Low Self** (*Unihipili, Ku* or Subconscious)
- **Middle Self** (*Uhane* or Conscious Mind), and
- **High Self** (*Aumakua,* Spirit or God)

The Low Self

This self – also called **Unihipili** - was, according to Long, made of Polynesian root words for "spirit" "grasshopper" and "leg and arm bones." In digging further, he discovered that these terms were descriptive metaphors for certain "powers" exhibited by this self.

Among them, Long described the ability of the Low Self

- to know itself as a **separate conscious spirit,**
- **provide life force**, or "mana" to all three selves, and
- to become **subject to hypnotic suggestions** and commands from the middle self or conscious mind.

According to Long, the Low Self or *Ku* also governed

- the **body** (except for the voluntary muscles),
- the **emotions,**
- the **memory,**
- all **sensory** impressions
- all telepathic and **psychic** abilities.

In fact, so much of the body and the emotions and the memory was tied up in this being that the *Kahunas* considered it the guardian of **Mana** (or "*life force*" or strong emotional charge). This *Mana* was shared with the Middle Self (conscious mind) which converted it into *will* or *intent.*

The Low Self also had the unique ability to contact the High Self through **"prayer."** The middle self or conscious mind is unable to do this – only make suggestions to the low self. For example, if a prayer is contrary to a previously-establish command by the middle self (e.g., childhood hidden decision), then the prayer would not be sent or heard.

The Low Self is so powerful that I originally called it *"The One Who Makes Things Happen"* before I discovered Long's books. This self, "inner child," *Ku,* or *Unihipli,* is the one we communicate with, through muscle testing.

The Middle Self

This entity is what we normally considered as our "self" or ego. According to the *Kahuna*, however, this same self is practically powerless without its servant, the *Ku*. The **middle self** was labeled by the *Kahunas* as **Uhane,** or "the spirit which talks."

Besides the ability to form words and speak, the middle self also has the ability to rationalize, solve puzzles, think logically, and – most importantly of all – **make decisions.** This ability above all others makes the *Uhane* the captain of this ship we call "our life," and guide to its destiny.

The limitations of the middle self, however, are many. It cannot get input from its surroundings, remember anything, or feel anything without the help of the low self. By itself it is a ghost, a wandering apparition, with no memory of its past or knowledge of its environment.

The middle self also lacks the ability to pray for what it wants. All it can do is make a request of the low self who then transmits this as a "prayer" to the High Self to "rain down benefits."

The High Self

Aumakua means in Polynesian *"utterly trustworthy parental spirit."* It is equivalent in meaning to the Judeo-Christian "Father in Heaven" and "Great Spirit" of the Native Americans. To the *Kahunas* it is the ultimate creator of all things in Heaven and Earth.

The High Self manifests all things, seen and unseen, on earth and in the cosmos. The middle self, however, has no direct contact with this Being. It must go through the low self to accomplish this. Only the low self can extend it's "aka cord" or ectoplasmic thought substance to the High Self in the form of a prayer.

According to Long:

> *If the three selves are working normally and freely together, the low self – at the request of the middle self – can at any time call up the High Self by way of the aka cord and give it a message.* [17]

Long's "prayer" therefore becomes a dance between the three selves, to the benefit of all. *Nothing happens unless all three are in harmony – together!*

How The Magic Was Lost

Freud and modern psychology have given us the knowledge of three divisions of consciousness, i.e., the **id** (subconscious), **ego** (conscious), and **superego.** While this knowledge was light years ahead of anything we knew before, it still treats the three "selves" as **parts** of one consciousness we call the *"individual"* – or undivided being.

We have **the Greeks** and other western cultures to thank for this idea. By elevating the individual as Hero, the Greeks, Romans and early church, created an ignorance of human interconnectedness, and a kind of arrogance that said we could do things without any real inner guidance. This growing reliance on outward signs, i.e., the word of the church, prophesies or divination, forestalled our search for inner awareness and divine power.

In fact, before Freud we westerners could never conceptualize what the ancient *Kahunas* meant by "three selves." *Kahuna* references to "selves" sounded like mere idol worship to early Hawaiian Christian missionaries of the early 1800's.

This was our loss. The missionaries – and western society itself - had much to gain from the *Kahunas.* Instead, they burned all their materials and sacred objects from that time. Long pointed out:

> *The idea of one supreme God was the Hebrew contribution to the world's thought on this subject. But in doing this masterly bit of reasoning, the reasoners accomplished for many branches of religion the wiping out of every level or form of consciousness between the middle self and Ultimate God, leaving a vast emptiness . . .* [18]

Ancient Hawaiian history was lost. The only resources Max Freedom Long could find were a few natives who were able to re-construct some folk stories, and the Polynesian language itself. But re-construct he did, and we owe Mr. Long a huge debt of gratitude.

Huna and the Logical Soul®

The practice of the *Logical Soul*® in fact, owes a great debt to *Huna.* When I first began to experiment with the "body spirit" as a **separate entity** or being, instead of merely as *the subconscious,* I began to get answers I never got

The Logical Soul®

before. Some mysterious force (the low self or *Ku*) was yearning to reveal its secrets to one who would actually listen . . . and actually *respect* the intelligence within.

It all began to make sense: The body and memory all lie within the realm of the *Ku*. I therefore addressed the *Ku* as a separate and unique being, and allowed it to respond to me as such. Over time I was then informed that the *Ku* is more than willing to accommodate ANY command by the conscious mind, *so long as that command does NOT run counter to a previous command already in place.*

This is because the low self will pray to the High Self for only those things it has been directed – with the greatest intent and force of emotion – to pray for. The conscious mind/middle self only has a say-so when it is clear and does not contradict itself, now or from past instructions. And remember, the *Ku never forgets a command!*

I liken this whole process to riding a whale. A whale (High Self) has its own consciousness; its own power, and obeys commands and instructions given by the riders - the middle and low selves. Both you and your *Ku* are riding this whale, but only the *Ku* (low self) has the power to direct this whale, based on your conscious instructions.

And the whale doesn't care. It will go anywhere it is directed.

If (and when) you gave the *Ku* (and subsequently the whale) specific and powerful directions very early in the journey, i.e., as a small child, this then became the whale's **prime directive.** All subsequent directions would also be followed – so long as the prime directive was not opposed.

In other words, we are like little beings riding on top of this whale. We tap it over here and tell it to go over here, then tap there to go in a different direction. So long as there's no conflict, that whale will gladly go in that direction.

If there is a conflict, i.e., if there is a *strong prime directive* to go in <u>another</u> direction, the *Ku* will direct this whale in <u>that</u> direction instead, *regardless* of our conscious wishes, hopes and fears.

That's how and why goal-to-action conflicts arise. We are "riding" this whale - in essence, a very large and powerful being that is *determined* to take us where we originally told it to go. While only the middle self or conscious mind can make decisions, the *Ku* controls the direction AND is not listening! Based on its memory of the original prime directive, the *Ku* stays the course.

If we want or need to change that directive, *we must have the right access and tools.* We must develop the ability to communicate to the *Ku* and get access to earlier decisions or directives. Only then will we be able to re-direct the whale.

The *Logical Soul®* process is about getting **access** to that decision that both the *Ku* and *Aumakua* see as their prime directive. Their outcome is set. How do you know what this is? Simple; it's where you are right now!

In essence, the idea of where and who you ARE is based on the decisions that you've made: ancient decisions; hidden decisions you made that have led you to this point. To be able to *change* those decisions, something very deep has to take place – communication with that being, whom the *Kahunas* call the *Ku* or Low Self. Only he has access to that "whale," our source of power.

We have to be able to say *"Look, you know, um, we're like, heading over the precipice! Can we, like, change directions a little??"* The whale will not do this just on a whim. It will not do what you say just because you say so. It will, however, listen to the *Ku* when *this being* becomes convinced there's something at stake - *something that relates to his original prime directive.*

And that something is your "inner child" or memory of the one whose decision set this whale on its original path, i.e.

The one who made the original decision is the only one who can change the decision.

So if this inner being (*Ku*) was listening to the conscious mind (*Uhane*) of you as a child of three years old, then it will also listen to this same child change the decision . . . if he is approached properly.

That's the secret of *Logical Soul®*. The key element is that we always go to the one who made the decision, get access to that event, to that person;

allow them to change the decision, and _then_ the prime directive transforms itself into a new decision.

CHAPTER TWELVE

How to Empower Your Affirmations

"The real voyage of discovery consists not in seeking new lands, but in seeing with new eyes."
- Marcel Proust

The following excerpts are from a 2008 video E-Class from www.logicalsoul.com:

Michael: Hi, I'm **Michael Craig.** I want to talk about how we're going to add power to your affirmations. I've asked my wife **Brigitte Soma** to join me, and we are going to demonstrate how this works with *The Logical Soul®*, so that you can try this at home and test members of your family, your friends, spouse, and so forth.

It is very important to know the process. I'll be going over the process in more detail in future lessons, but for right now, let's see how **affirmations** play into this process and how we can use them.

First thing is, thank you Brigitte for joining me. What I want to do is show the folks how to muscle test. We went over how to self-test using the fingers and so forth but I want to use you as a real example to show people how we can muscle test.

The first thing to do is to raise the arm to the horizontal, or parallel to the ground - straight out basically - and have the person just lock their shoulder into place. Now, that doesn't mean they're fighting you; it shouldn't be a contest. So you want to have the person just lock their shoulder.

The next thing is to press on the wrist of the person using about three fingers. Ask the person to hold – hold - so you feel that lock into place, right? Okay. Now, if you have to push on it then that's not what we are talking about. We're not talking about a strength contest. We're talking about whether or not this person is locking their shoulder. Hold.

Now let's do a trial test of this. Say *"my name is George."*

Brigitte: My name is George.

Michael: Hold. Okay. There's a little bit of a . . . of course . . . she went and blew out. But the point is that it will become a little bit weaker. It may not be totally weak, but it may become a little bit what I call rubbery. If it's rubbery, that's a weak muscle and that's called "muscle testing" or "Applied Kinesiology."

So you can test affirmations using this technique. The main thing is to make a positive statement. Usually though, it involves a choice, something to do with **intent** because those are the most powerful affirmations that you can use - those having to do with intent.

Because you may make an affirmation and say, well, I'm not happy or I'm happy or not happy, and that may be what is called a condition. A "condition" is different than "intent." What we want to do is have an intent which would be what? I choose to be happy, right? So let's make a statement of intent, such as *"I choose to be happy."*

Brigitte: I choose to be happy.

Michael: Hold. Okay. So that works. Let's just use for an example something that a lot of us come face-to-face with, relationships or money. How about money and gifts? What

I found is a lot of people can't accept things. And even though they may want to earn and make money, I found a lot of people cannot accept things.

Maybe you can ask yourself this question too - whether or not you can accept money or gifts. Let's just test for gifts. Now, we integrated her (Brigitte) for this particular statement so she should be strong on that. Let's just check and see if that's the case. Say *"I choose to accept money and gifts."*

Brigitte: I choose to accept money and gifts.

Michael: Hold. Alright. Now, she's strong on that. That wasn't always the case, was it?

Brigitte: No.

Michael: Actually, you had a situation where you couldn't accept, what, several years ago, back in the '90s; and then we worked on that and that was one of the major pieces that we got into place bringing that into being . . .

Brigitte: Right.

Michael: So if this were... Let's make that statement, again, *"I can easily accept money and gifts."*

Brigitte: I can easily accept money and gifts.

Michael: Now, just for demonstration purposes, go a little weak on that. Okay, so if the muscle gets weak, then what we do is find out whether or not there's **access to change this program** . . . the program being the affirmation. Say, *"Access is available to change this program."*

Brigitte: Access is available to change this program.

Michael: Hold. All right. If access is available, that means your conscious mind can change it. In other words, your conscious mind has access to get in there and change that affirmation or that particular program.

If it does *not* have access, there's a whole other procedure, which I'll go into in future lessons, about how to get access. But for right now, let's just assume we *do* have access. The next step would be to address this being - or *Ku* – as if it were separate from your conscious mind, which in most cases it is. The statement would be, *"I allow Brigitte access to change this program."* Say that.

Brigitte: I allow Brigitte access to change this program.

Michael: Hold. So she's strong on that, too. So first of all, we find out whether or not access is even available. Sometimes it's not even available. And then we find out whether our conscious mind, our adult mind, has access to get in there and change that.

This can be done also, by the way, with children. When I say adult mind, I assume who I'm speaking to is adult. But also it works with kids, as well.

If access is available to change it, the next thing is to close the eyes. Go back to the very first time you *remember* having to turn down – or not accept - money and gifts, for whatever reason. It may not be the first time, but the first time you remember.

Brigitte: Okay.

Michael: Great. And then she'll have some memory or situation come up . . . in fact, you did have a situation. What was that? Do you want to tell the story of what happened?

Brigitte: I was five years old and I went to the shop to buy something not far away from home. It was four minutes, walking time. And there was a mother with another kid, and the kid wanted my toy.

I said, *"Well, you can have my toy, but it will cost you five German marks."* Her mother was so disgusted with me wanting money for the gift that she went to my mother and said how impossible I was to ask for money. My mother agreed - I was really, really bad to even *ask* for money.

So that was locked in. I would not ask for money; I would not take money. I thought it's bad and evil and...

Michael: Very good. Whatever your story is about money, a lot of times it will get locked into place. We're just using this as an example, by the way. There are so many different things that come up for us.

Money is one of the big issues that people are faced with, so it comes up quite a lot. Are you able to accept money? If not, test yourself. If you can't accept money or gifts, check to see whether access is available to change this program. Or find out if your conscious mind has access and if that is, then go back to the very first time that you remember having this experience, walk yourself through it.

The technique I use to reinforce that information is have your adult self go back to that incident just as it happened and see yourself at that place, where the child is having difficulty accepting. Then turn around and talk to the adults that are responsible for that programming and tell them off. Tell them exactly what they need to hear, what you needed to hear as a child. Become that child's champion.

Also have the child tell them what he or she thinks about all this. Very important - the one who made the decision can change the decision. So if your child made that decision that accepting money is bad, <u>the child must then make a new decision.</u> So whoever made the decision can also change it, if access is available.

And, again, we'll go into a process where we'll find out how to change if access is not available. But for right now, you can change a lot of things in your life, just by doing this simple exercise.

We take a few minutes, feel that change in our bodies, come out, and count ourselves out, which basically is take a deep breath and then open your eyes. So then we retest the body. Say, "I can accept money and gifts easily."

Brigitte: I can accept money and gifts easily.

Michael: Hold. And she's strong. There was a time when she was not strong on that, which means that the statement was false. Right now it's true. So you feel that change in your life that you're able to accept things now?

Brigitte: Very much.

Michael: I can vouch for that. She loves it when I give her things. And thank you for being part of this session today. Thank you and I look forward to our next class.

CHAPTER THIRTEEN

How to Deal with Criticism and Failure

"I saw my soul in a deep dark hole and then I followed it in..."
- Kenny Rogers lyric

The Feeling in Your Gut

How do you deal with criticism or failure in your life?

Does it make you downtrodden? Sad? Do you get angry? Do you feel really upset? Does it stop your enthusiasm and movement toward your goals? Or do you just push it off and move on?

These are important considerations - how you handle criticism and how you handle failure. In fact, this single factor is <u>the basis of your success</u>. Your ability to rebound from certain failure – not the failure itself – determines whether or not you are a winner.

That doesn't mean you have to fail constantly to be successful, no. But **failure is inherent in success** . . . just as stumbling is inherent in learning to walk. Everybody does it; everybody fails. Therefore <u>the only barrier to success is giving up!</u>

My life followed this pattern for years and years, because I failed more times than I succeeded; in fact *many* more times. In the beginning of these failures I was totally crushed. Defeated. I had this feeling inside like somebody had punched me in the stomach; did it to me personally. Each failure became like a personal cross I had to bear . . . and it hurt. I mean, failure *absolutely hurts* in the beginning.

While I realized that most of the problem was inside me, that knowledge didn't help. There was something there, inside myself; inside my gut that *just did not allow me to move forward.*

Affirmations, success training, writing down and repeating goals, and *rah-rah* seminars and other motivational training only served to add to my despair once the smoke had cleared & reality set in.

It took me most of my life to discover exactly what this *"seed of failure"* was and how to dig it out. The reason was that this seed – like that which sprouts and grows into a kudzu plant in the southern United States – was extremely powerful and resistant (*Riddle:* How do you grow Kudzu? *Answer:* Throw the seeds on the ground, fertilize them with concrete blocks, and run like heck before it grows all over you!). All the affirmations and goal-setting in the world was not going to dislodge *this* sucker!

The Seeds of Failure & Success

We are born with both seeds of failure and success. One, however, is dominant. Maybe it became dominant in the first few years of our life. Maybe it became dominant through ancestral tendencies. I don't know. What I *do* know, however, is that <u>most</u> people are either born with, or develop at an early age, the tendency to fail. *Innate success is a rare gift.*

By the way, the root or **Seed of Failure (SOF)** is NOT the same failure spoke of by the Great Ones – the masters of Achievement and high-income earners and producers. Most of their failures – though many – had to do with **circumstances,** or outside obstacles and barriers. They still had their emotional/mental **Seed of Success (SOS)** firmly planted, even if it might have started out rather small.

Different "success gurus" report different trials and tribulations, i.e., arriving in the US "with a buck-fifty in my pocket;" "sleeping in my apartment bathtub;" "selling vacuum cleaners door-to-door" and other delightful memories only strengthened their resolve (or SOS) to achieve unbelievable success in later life. One with SOS, in fact, *uses* all these failure stories to actually lay the foundation for his or her later success.

In the beginning of my search for success I even took a page from their book. I started documenting all my humble circumstances in the hope that this exercise would spur me to greater success as well. It didn't. After a decade of writing all this stuff down, however, nothing changed. I finally decided to ditch the whole thing after the stack of sob stories got too depressing to look at!

It took some very subtle stealth tactics and quite a bit of grace (and maybe a touch of luck) to be able to access my own *Seed of Failure* and render it impotent. I'm sharing this with you in the hope that you won't have to repeat what I went through, along with countless others.

If you're young, that's great. You can take this information now and use it to expand your SOS exponentially. If you're older, you will have a deeper appreciation of the fact that this method is more effective than *any* affirmation or motivational program you've tried before.

Failure Has a Very Good Reason

Your ability to succeed is based on your poise in failure and your poise under fire, under criticism. How you handle failure and how you succeed are two sides of the same coin.

When you fail, you either learn to let it go . . . or it sets up housekeeping in your physiology, your gut, your abdomen, your heart, and your head. Something happens where, physiologically speaking, failure sets in.

Now, if you are sensitive, chances are you've learned how to just feel the wave of disappointment and let it go. But the negative thoughts – some experts refer to them as **mind viruses**[19]:

- **Persist *in spite of*** your willingness to let them go.

- **Persist *in spite of*** your willingness to relax and release them.

- **Persist *in spite of*** all the positive affirmations you can conjure, and

- **Persist *in spite of*** coaches, mentors, and gurus guiding your way.

They persist because, quite frankly, you're convinced you are a failure, and there is a ***very good reason*** for remaining a failure! This hidden set of reasons, or SOF, is the same as the *prime directive* we spoke of earlier. It must be obeyed - *in spite of* any and all attempts to counter it.

The **self-talk** that arises from the Seed of Failure is also persistent. This inner chatter sets up housekeeping in the head and continues to spout its wisdom to us every few minutes.

We attempt to root out the negative self-talk through positive goal setting, through affirmations; through hypnosis; and through any other means we know of, in order to get rid of the self-talk, or to make the

positive self-talk so much *louder* that the negative just sort of disappears.

And to a degree, that works. To a large degree, however, it does *not* work. Most self-talk is based on decisions made very early in life, often before we can remember learning to talk. Repeating "every day in every way I am getting better and better" does little good, for example, to heal a gaping hole in your gut caused by an abusive family member.

And what do you do with that type of self-talk that is so deep it's anchored into your physiology at birth or soon after birth? Sometimes even before birth?? This type of self-talk is not self-talk at all because it's *pre-language.*

All self-talk is based on a **decision,** however. Maybe it was made on an organic level - just like an amoeba makes a decision to back away from pain or stimulus. We make decisions, even in the womb, even shortly after birth, that we back away from pain. We back away from discomfort.

These types of decisions, which I call **organic decisions,** are anchored into the physiology and have just as much to do with our success and our ability to handle failure as anything else. But organic or not, let's take a few minutes to investigate the *Logical Soul*® method I used to reveal these underlying decisions – the Root of Failure - whatever the source.

Major Decision: Are You Open or Closed?

I used to hear the argument during some of my talks *"But why should I focus on failure?"* they asked. *"All I want to do is stay positive!"*

I would usually nod my head in understanding, *and* respond.

"Thanks for the question. Now, while yours is a wonderful objective, it doesn't work" I added. *"The fact is . . . if all this staying positive stuff* DID *work, everyone who ever made a goal and affirmation would succeed, would they not?"*

"But aren't you defeating the purpose of trying to achieve goals by focusing on the negative?" Their words suddenly gave me an idea for an analogy.

"Let's say you're driving down the road headed to a concert," I proposed, *"and your car started smoking from the hood. You know it's probably the radiator, so you stop to check and maybe pour in some more water before your engine burns up."*

"Now your goal is the concert. Using your example, I should ignore the smoke and continue to stay focused on arriving at the concert.

"There's a name for people like this: I call them 'pedestrians.'"

By this time, folks usually laughed a little and started listening a little more intently.

"Look at it this way," I continued, *"you are* ALREADY *negative. You just don't know where that negative part lives inside you. Better to contact it, change it and implant the positive rather than live your life in a fog of denial!"*

At this point, some people would shift in their chairs, indicating they would prefer to stay "positive" despite any signals to the contrary. That's OK. The ones who truly heard the message later told me my talk opened their eyes. Those who chose to stay open-minded received a real benefit.

The others? They merely got to be right.

Are you still with me? Great! The next chapter will describe the process I use to discover the source of hidden decisions that lead to pain.

CHAPTER FOURTEEN

How to Discover Your Seed of Failure

*"Success has a hundred parents.
Failure is an orphan."*
- John R. Ashton

The Hidden Critic

Usually when I'm doing sessions with clients or patients, it's all based on conversation and instant feedback. When you are doing this work from home, however, it might help you to write down detailed descriptions of your current problem or issue. Then stop and *feel* how this problem is in your body.

Let's say, for instance that you have a general *feeling* of failure. Begin to list or itemize the **cost** of this failure, e.g., what it has cost you in terms of loss of money, loss of respect from your family and others; disappointment, fear, and descent into a world of unhappiness and irrelevance.

Once this feeling is at its peak, notice the effect on your body. Where is the tightness? Then ask a thought to arise within you that represents this feeling . . . pull out of your mental/emotional file <u>the very first time you remember failing or being criticized</u>. Feel the energy surrounding that failure. Notice the stress in your body.

If the emotion is at a peak – and the feeling is present in the body – look for some **statement** to arise. Look to see if something comes to mind that *summarizes* this anger, fear, disappointment, humiliation or regret. If so, verbalize it. Write it down. What statement would make you want to lash out at something? Be angry at something?

If nothing arises, just be with the feeling for awhile. *Be patient.*

Remember, this has been with you, like, *forever.* Wait for some thought to come up having to do with the *very first time you remember* feeling this failure, feeling this anger; feeling this inability to succeed, whatever reason. This is because you had that same feeling at one point and the memory still resides in your body and nervous system.

The earliest *remembered* feeling (and corresponding thought) that comes up is usually tied with some judgment or decision you made about that experience. This would be a decision tied to the Seed of Failure for this particular issue.

In other words, you may have been criticized when you were very small.

The Logical Soul®

How I Lost the Store

I remember as a small child – around nine or ten - I had this general store that I built out of cardboard. I put it up in my front yard and sold comic books and candy to the neighborhood kids that I'd collected while Halloween trick-or-treating.

Business was good. A week after Halloween, most neighborhood kids have already used up their stash and started to feel withdrawal symptoms from the sugar crash. Consequently, my store was the center of town for many of them. Since I didn't have much of a sweet tooth at the time, so I still had my stash sitting around, ready to meet the fresh demand.

I was real proud of my cardboard store. I was a little kid acting all grown up and being a business person. The great part was, I was actually succeeding! I made more money than I got from an allowance, and it was *all profit* since my inventory was free.

One day my dad walks up to me, playing the role of government agent I suppose, and fires a couple of loaded questions at me:

> "Do you have a business license?"
> "Are you going to file your tax returns and pay taxes?"

Now, my dad was the kind of guy who loved to kid around. Trouble was, I was too innocent to understand when he was kidding and when he wasn't! I therefore felt some pressure to answer – *but did not know the answer!*

While his questions bounced around in my head, I sat there looking dumbfounded until my dad simply shrugged and walked off. I breathed a sigh of relief, but the questions haunted me.

What is obvious to me now was that he was kidding. *As a child, however, it had a deep affect on me.* If he *were* serious – and I got the answer *wrong* (I reasoned) – I might get a spanking. I therefore felt shocked and shut down. I didn't have what he was talking about. I also had *no* idea the things he spoke of, how to get them, or what would happen to me in my ignorance!

For years and years after that, I remained shut down. I closed my store and contented myself with "safer" projects like reading, building stuff and hanging out with one or two close friends.

I had made the decision "I don't know enough. I'm not prepared." Eventually I forgot the incident.

My body, however, did not forget about it. It was in my physiology. I spent the rest of my life trying to overcompensate for what I felt was my profound ignorance on such matters. I learned how to set up corporations. I even studied the *Internal Revenue Code* and regulations in case I had to tangle with the IRS, for Pete's sake!

When my physiology became involved at that critical age of ten, everything that I did from then on was somehow connected to that failure to please my

Dad. In this sense, it also became a general decision that he would always know more than I did – something I was unable to shed until years after his death.

I took my Dad's kidding a certain way. As kids, we take a lot of things a certain way. Failure sinks deep into our physiology, simply because we don't yet have the conscious tools needed to interpret events correctly. I took the words *"not having a business license"* and made up a story about how I'm not smart enough, and the hidden decisions that were spawned by this feeling.

Steps to Discovery

The way to discover your own seed of failure is to first feel it inside your gut, then do a few things to change the hidden decision about it. Here are some simple steps you can take to start out:

- Close your eyes.
- Go back to the very first time you remember feeling that way.
- Listen for the decision about that particular feeling.
- Write it down.

The next step is to create a statement or affirmation that is the opposite of your negative one. *"I choose to fail in business,"* for example might be *"I choose to succeed in business,"* or whatever it is.

Then muscle test the positive statement. If *"I choose to succeed"* goes weak, then you've hit on at least part of your Seed of Failure.

At this point, return to the *first time you remember* feeling where that statement was NOT true. That thought, that decision that you made, is the thought you need to work with. *That* is the decision that can be changed.

In the next chapter I'm going to start revealing the entire Logical Soul® process – how I do most session *in 30 minutes or less!* With it, you will be able to quickly *question, discover, access,* and *resolve* practically any problem or pressing issue.

CHAPTER FIFTEEN

The Interview

"I would never join any club that would have me as a member."
- Groucho Marx

A Simple Technique

There are four phases of the *Logical Soul®* technique:

1. **Interview**
2. **Discovery**
3. **Access**
4. **Resolution**

Over this and the next three chapters, I'll be going over each phase in some detail. It's a natural progression; each phase naturally follows the one before it.

Keep in mind, however, that doing this process on others or yourself involves a lot of listening, a fair amount of intuition, a bit of skill in muscle testing or self-testing . . . *and* the rare ability to *get your ego out of the way.* If you have these necessary skills, go for it. If not, you may want to attend a *Logical Soul®* course or workshop to get these skills (see our website for details and schedules).

The first phase is the **Interview.** While during the first session it may be longer, the time needed is usually about **5-10 minutes.** It involves sitting with another person – assuming you are doing it with another person – asking certain questions and letting them talk. If you are doing this process by yourself, review the previous chapter so you will have an idea of how to "interview" yourself.

By the way, it's best to do this process with another person for two reasons:

1. You're not going to get the same honest feedback from yourself as you would with another person, and
2. It's just easier to muscle test with someone else.

Talking with another person also adds an extra dimension to our self-knowledge. Because we tend to have ideas about ourselves and the way we're going, it's very difficult to see ourselves the way others see us. Another person can have access to our inner motivation when we may not even realize it is there.

So have a second person - a partner, a spouse, a family member, a friend - who can go through this process with you. They should also be familiar with how the method works, and willing to work with you on a regular basis.

Don't know anyone like this? Find someone you think would be receptive, give them a copy of this book, and ask if they would work with you. Or form your own **Logical Soul® Meetup group** (see details at www.meetup.com) in your city or area. It is also a great way to develop lasting friendships.

Getting Started

Sit with the other person. Whether you know this person very well or not, be sure to first have an understanding of the purpose of this session: **to find, access, and change our hidden decisions** for greater success and happiness.

The interview is *not* about how we are doing, the weather, the news, what we are doing at work, how our life is going, or any of that stuff. It's about issues that we hardly ever talk about: our fears, anxieties, resentments and things that bog us down, or make us dull and ineffective.

[Important Note: It's also about seeing the other person as a *Divine Being* – one who has made inner decisions that is creating the world around them. Right now! As such, there is no "right" or "wrong"... and therefore, no need to "fix" them!]

While interviewing this person (it could be a male or female, but for purposes of this exercise I will stick with the masculine pronoun), ask him

The Logical Soul®
"What issue is up for you today?"

Now, that's a very simple question, but it has a very important component to it. By asking what is up for him *"today"* (or *"now"*) he begins to focus on how his body feels. In other words, he observes what is happening in his body or mind that is causing a concern right this minute.

Most people have some issue at hand. Either it's money, relationships, health . . . *something* that's bothering them. And if something *is* bothering them, start asking questions about it.

Your main job, by the way, is to **listen.**

No one will talk – especially about deep-seated fears or concerns – if the person they are speaking to is yawning, looking at his watch, or glancing at the floor. This part, by the way, is the hardest thing for some people to do – saying *nothing* while another person talks.

The ego – based on the *Ku's* memories of early childhood - wants to be noticed; it wants to "do" a successful *Logical Soul®* interview. It wants to be the hero, the expert, the master.

The *Ku* is still trying to prove to Mommy and Daddy that it can do things all by itself. While we as adults know better, this programming keeps playing over and over again, subconsciously.

Just notice the feeling and let it go. The *Logical Soul®* process happens naturally by itself, but you must get out of the way. Put your ego aside for the time allotted and simply hold the space for the other person to speak and share. Again, there is nothing to "fix" and you are therefore engaged in what I call "Divine Listening."

Assuming you can do this, let's proceed . . .

The Five Why's

The Interview Phase is based on the **Socratic Method,** i.e., teaching by asking questions. If you're not used to doing that, a really helpful method for starting is to ask **five "why's"** in consecutive order.

Let's say your client or partner is concerned – as in our previous example - about money. His income is not so good. So the next question might be to him:

"Why do you think that is?"

He might then answer

> *"Well, my job really is, you know . . . I don't really like my job."*
>
> *"It's difficult . . . the boss is demanding."*
>
> *"A lot of things are happening in my life right now."*
>
> *"I just don't know what to do with so little money,"* and so forth.

Continue asking a similar "why" question *at least five times.* This allows for deeper self-reflection on the part of your client or partner. At some point, he or she may respond to the question, *"Well, why do you think that is?"* with *"I don't know."*

When you start getting into the "I-don't-knows" you enter a deeper realm of consciousness, closer to "The Wall." This is the place where the mind says emphatically "No more!" <u>You don't want to push,</u> but proceed as far as you can. Gently.

By the way, this level of persistent "I-don't-knows" - and it may be two or three questions in - is the level at which the *Logical Soul®* technique begins to become most helpful. When you can begin to make statements around that issue and find out from your **body** what is going on, then you can know exactly what is happening in the **mind** and how to change or overcome it. This part we will cover in the next few phases.

Begging the Question

The interview is, on the surface, just sitting and talking. In reality, however, this process is vitally important to find out and pinpoint **exactly what affirmation is needed** to use and test the body (in the Discovery Phase) to find out whether or not the key hidden decisions can be changed.

In addition to the five Why's, another method is to simply ask questions based on the answers provided at each step, or "begging the question."

For example, when you ask *"why do you think your boss is mean or your job is so demanding?"* they might respond by elaborating, *"Well, I really want to be a writer."*

That begs the question: *"What prevents you from being a writer?"* Then they might go into a whole statement about that.

If you keep asking enough questions, there will come a point at which the truth pops out: *"I don't believe I can make any money being a writer,"* or something similar.

Testing the Statement

Assuming the above example is the closest you can come to the truth, you might want to test it. The way you test a statement is to **reverse the negative statement** and turn it into several **affirmations** you can muscle test:

"I can make money being a writer."

"I choose to make money being a writer."

"I know how to make money being a writer," etc.

Once you begin the process, it changes and adapts to whatever comes up. The issue may actually be around money itself. Or creativity. Perhaps he was told when he was very young that he couldn't write, or something to that effect.

But, yet, it's inside of him, and it may take a *Logical Soul®* session or two to find this out. These questions and tests are crucial for that reason alone!

The interview is vitally important. Until you discover *what* statement to use and *where* the statement is directing a person's life, you won't be able to go to the next step: **Discovery.**

CHAPTER SIXTEEN

Discovery

*"If at first you don't succeed,
failure may be your style."*
- Quentin Crisp

The second part of the *Logical Soul®* process is called **Discovery**. Time needed: about **5-7 minutes** or longer, depending on your level of expertise.

The Importance of Instant Feedback

Once you have a statement or affirmation, the next step is to test it and to **find out *exactly* where the feelings and decisions come from** that either

> a) **support it,** or
> b) **reject it.**

Discovery is the process we begin when we've reached the "I-don't-knows," remember? It's the point at which muscle testing becomes crucial. The body will begin to give us answers about the "why" and the "why not" of any given statement.

It is also crucial for giving *instant feedback* as proof to the one being tested. In our mind, when we see the muscle going weak we know we have hit on something important for our partner. With weakness there is lack of congruence – lack of inner strength. And we also know this can be strengthened.

In our partner's mind, feeling his muscle going weak sends a message to his brain, both conscious and subconscious, saying:

"I'm lying to myself,"

"I'm not truthful with myself,"

"I'm wasting my time doing things I once thought I could do."

This alone is a very powerful transforming event for most people.

If you can experience this yourself, that's OK, but not ideal. With a partner it's a little harder to fib your way through it, and is much more powerful. Having a partner to work with throughout this process allows you the freedom to focus on your statements themselves, and less on whether or not you are doing it right.

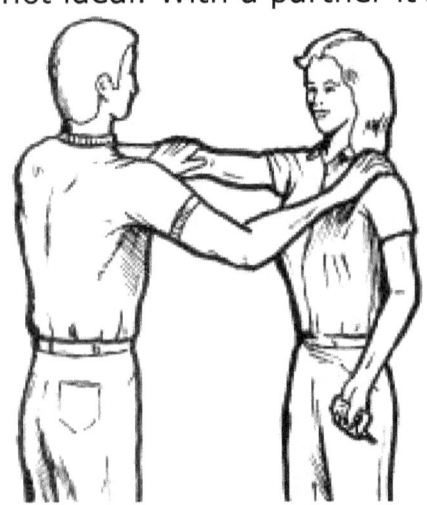

Also, using a partner fulfills the biblical

injunction *"when two or more are gathered in my name, there I be also."* There's power in numbers.

During testing you'll find there are a lot of things in your life you *thought* were true that turn out to be false. You may also find out there are a lot of thoughts, feelings, ideas, dreams and affirmations that you *thought* were right on target, but turn out to be *false ideals* because your *hidden decisions* were sabotaging all attempts to make them happen!

Such is the power of instant feedback!

Hey, I'm Not So Sure About This Testing...

You might have questions at this point, such as:

> *"Well, how do I know you're not pushing harder?"*
>
> *"How do I know this really works?"*
>
> *"Why should I trust this?"*

Fair questions. Each of them has an answer (see below), but also consider this: have you spent a lot of time in your life breaking things down and tearing things apart to see if they are "real"?

If so, maybe you've also heard the story of the golden goose . . . Some greedy villagers cut the poor animal open to find out *how* she laid all those golden eggs, and behold! Now they can't get any more eggs AND they are no closer to finding out "the truth" about how she laid them.

Yes, I know it's a fairy tale. I also know that muscle testing works, AND it will work in the presence of those who allow a "yes" to be a part of their vocabulary and their lives. If you are too critical it will not work for you; and

you will actually prove yourself right every time. Consider, then, using more objective methods of testing such as a **polygraph** or **CVSA** (see p. 144).

Before giving up on muscle testing entirely, however, consider that you have nothing to lose by being neutral about the whole thing. So why not try it out? It's common sense based on risk/reward. What have you *really* got to lose if it actually works?? Nothing. It's the cheapest tool you will find to yield the greatest possible reward – peace of mind.

To answer your questions, here are some thoughts:

You're pushing harder. Depending on your partner, most will *not* have an agenda or stake in whether or not your answers are "yes" or "no". If they do, work with someone else. Once you set up the test statements, however, and get a neutral yes/no with slight pressure, the rest should easily follow suit and the results will be accurate. It is common, however, for you to get tired, especially after a long session. In that case, rest or use the other arm.

Does A.K. really work? Applied Kinesiology was formulated in the 1960's by a chiropractor, **Dr. George Goodheart,** as a tool for testing the viability of muscles in different stresses and circumstances. He discovered that muscles "hold" when both the inner and outer environments are supportive to the subject being tested.

During the years since, thousands of medical doctors, chiropractors, therapists, CIA agents and others have used muscle testing for both therapeutic and lie-detection purposes. Many of their findings have been verified by the use of instruments like electronic dynamometers, polygraph and other means.

For our purposes the use of A.K. in the *Logical Soul®* is not intended for therapeutic use, but as an experimental feedback tool only.

Why should I trust this? This is a question you might use to start delving into your own motivation. *If trust is an issue, obviously there have been disappointments.*

My own experience with gurus, goal-setting, affirmations, and self-improvement techniques led me to dismiss most of what I came across. At some point I realized, however, that critics like me don't accomplish much of anything in this world, and trust was not the *real* issue.

My real issue was *anger at myself* and embarrassment for *blindly trusting* people or things to be the perfect solution for me, then getting let down when this proved not to be the case. In other words, I set myself up for failure, then used that as "proof" that I couldn't trust people.

The perfect solution does <u>not</u> exist, and neither muscle testing nor the *Logical Soul®* is a panacea. They are, however, very useful tools for uncovering hidden decisions and bringing greater inner strength and peace of mind. Try the method on for size. You might be pleasantly surprised.

Using the Voice for Testing

If you have tried the muscle testing and still need some machine to tell you the truth, there is a way to do this. One promising technology I've found to approximate the use of simple muscle testing is **Computerized Voices Stress Analysis,** or **CVSA**.

CVSA is considered experimental, as are most "lie-detector" techniques, but is based on the principle that your voice changes when you come under a stress, such as lying. Law enforcement agencies and international airports are using this technique more and more over the traditional polygraph because it has proven to be less expensive, less invasive, and often more accurate.

How this approach compares to AK, I don't know. The biggest advantage of muscle testing is *zero cost* and *universal availability.* And while CVSA is much more expensive, less available, and produces probably the same accuracy, its big advantage is that *sessions can be done over the phone* more accurately with greater objectivity.

This is a brand new field of research waiting for more researchers. Do a Google search online for more information on this interesting new tool.

The Truth

Throughout the discovery process, you can determine whether or not a statement is "true" or "not true." These statements are never true on an absolute level, because there's no such thing as "absolute truth" according to modern science, physics, biology and mathematics.

What we are discovering in this phase, actually, is *whether or not something is* **true for you** *or* **not true for you.** That's all. And regardless of the answer, it's going to save you a lot of time, a lot of money, and a lot of heartaches, headaches, efforts and frustrations later on.

So the "truth" about you and money, as per our previous example, is that through muscle testing you can determine your hidden capacity for earning, accepting, and keeping money or gifts:

> *"I'm worth* [a certain amount of money]," or
> "I can accept gifts and money", or
> "I can accept [a certain amount of money]"
> and
> *"I can easily act on earning* [a certain amount of money]"

I've even refined it to where a certain amount of money can be reached. Through muscle testing we can actually measure the levels that you can accept, at which you can earn, at what you think you're worth.

The Logical Soul®

It is the last piece – "acting on" – that was missing from my earlier equation. Its addition made a HUGE difference in how the other statements actually manifested. Without it, the others had no traction!

You set the levels. You can repeat the process until you reach a higher and higher level at which you feel comfortable for owning, accepting, earning and acting on money and possessions. When the affirmation becomes true for you, i.e., you feel it inside and your body is saying "yes," you can go as high as you want.

CHAPTER SEVENTEEN

Access

"The person who takes resolution and then works diligently towards its fulfillment is helped and blessed by gods. He gets easy access to all the means necessary to success, growth and prosperity."
- Atharva Veda

The third phase of the *Logical Soul®* process is called **Access.** Time needed: about **5-8 minutes.**

What *Is* Access?

Access is really the *heart* of the *Logical Soul®*. It is what makes The *Logical Soul®* different than other self-improvement and goal-setting techniques out there.

Access is a way of getting beyond what I call **"The Wall"** - that thing you hit when you can't go any deeper inside. Every other technique I've ever seen or used has run up against – been confounded by - this wall. It's that subconscious barrier that stops us from getting the answers we really seek.

You see, when you set goals for your personal and business lives, most of your attention is invested in the idea that you must put forth a lot of positive thinking and effort to get there.

A lot of that effort, however, is used in fighting that wall; fighting those subconscious tendencies you have that sabotage your goals and affirmations in countless creative ways.

Decisions you made when you were very young – now hidden - keep you stuck in a box of insular thinking. This insular thinking sets up a limited **paradigm** (or worldview) that keeps you from seeing or understanding anything outside that box. Once in place, this paradigm is hard to change.

Paradigm Surfing

Examples of shifting paradigms can be seen everyday with the onslaught of new technologies. My paradigm for voice communication, for example has always been the phone. As a 60-something year old man I *still* think of a phone, whether it be rotary, pushbutton, cord, cordless, or cell, as just that – a *telephone.*

My 32-year old couch-surfing business consultant, on the other hand, sees it as a phone, calculator, computer, camera, organizer, rolodex, texting machine, and universal *Twitter-do-all-and-be-all thingee.* While he sends probably 60 texts a day, I've probably sent a grand total of five a *year!* If I want to reach a wider audience, I know I'll have to learn to take a deep breath and just "surf" with the dude.[20]

There is also the story I heard about the time when Darwin's ship **The Beagle** sailed into a closed harbor at **Patagonia** on the southern tip of South America.[21] The Europeans observed that the natives did not see them or the ship until they disembarked into longboats and headed to the shore. Suddenly the natives shouted and saw them!

Apparently, since such a large ship had never been seen by them before, their *paradigm* did not allow for them to comprehend such an entity. But they did recognize the men in longboats – a site more in alignment with their worldview.

Your Personal Paradigms

While you may hold many paradigms, your **personal story** is your major catch-all paradigm. It tells you what is true and what is false. It keeps you safe, and tells you what is OK and what is not.

Your personal story has been *your greatest single tool for survival* in this world . . . and *it's also based on lies!*

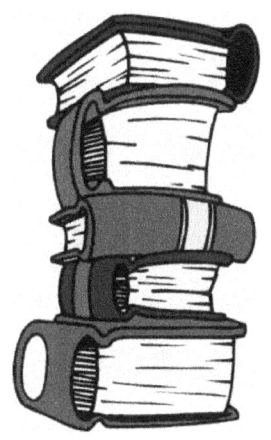

For the most part, *your personal story is a collection of beliefs and ideas rooted in decisions you made up about reality a long time ago.* The problems only come in when what you *think* is the truth is actually just your *story* about what you experienced.

And most people have this. Let's face it, when it comes to a choice between the truth and our story, we choose the story. Why? Because it's *OUR truth,* dammit!

So, in this way you keep your personal story in place. There is also not much room for change. There's not much room to grow. Only those decisions that fit into the neat little cubbyholes you've built for yourself are welcome.

All the other things will fall to the wayside. If you have difficulty attracting money and repeat "I can become a millionaire," "I choose to be a millionaire," or whatever, the truth of these statements won't hold up. Your universal paradigm, your personal story, is not geared to *accept* these particular affirmations or statements. They become – like the Beagle to the Patagonians – an invisible myth!

Through the *Interview* and *Discovery* phases, you learned a way to uncover which statements are "true" for you, and which are invisible to you. Supposedly you've discovered what I call **lynchpin decisions,** ones that hold many of the other, more superficial decisions in place.

Once you find out what these major underlying decisions are, the next step is to find out if you have **ACCESS** to them. Ask yourself:

"*Is access available?"* (to anyone, that is), and

"*Does my conscious mind have access to that?"* i.e., my adult self?

If you test for both of these (using declarative statements, not questions) and they test true, then we know you can change the underlying decision.

<u>If these statements are *not* true,</u> however, I have a process in the *Logical Soul®* where you can actually get to the other side. This is the *real key* to *The Logical Soul®* and the whole process takes about 10-15 minutes.

You can learn this powerful process and <u>change your life in minutes, not years.</u> You can get beyond "the Wall" and change what I call **archetypal decisions,** these key decisions at the very core of your essence, those key lynchpin decisions that govern who you are, and what the world is around you.

By changing these decisions, you unlock the <u>secret of how to convert the Seed of Failure (SOF) into the Seed of Success (SOS)</u>! THEN, all the success, motivational, and goal-setting courses start to make sense!!

When I first accomplished this breakthrough in 1992, the release was so powerful it took days for Cathy to come back to the point of stability. It now takes only minutes.

Back then I didn't know what I was doing, and daresay *nobody* knew how to do this. I happen to discover this by accident. And so it is by grace that I have this information and I'm passing this on to you.

Personal Guides and Archetypes

"Getting access," in a nutshell, means you ask the child or one who first made the decision. Then ask the child who he or she trusts more than anyone else

The Logical Soul®

in the whole universe. Once you discover that **trusted guide** or figure, they can open the door to let you in. Without the guide or trusted ally, there is no access.

This guide - your **personal archetype** - is the key to getting that access because that guide is the only one with access to the story and that child. Once access is gained, however, you can go in as an adult, have conversations with the guide and child, and ask them to change the limiting decision.

Again, **the one who made the decision can change the decision.** This person, child, or ancestor is the only who can do this. It is your *Ku* or low self and will not listen to your conscious pleas if they go against prime directives. So in order for the child (or someone else) to make a *new* decision, the guide or personal archetype must come in and accompany that child so that he or she feels **safe.**

This last step is critical to the whole process. The reason is because if the child does not feel safe, it cuts off access. There's an aspect of safety involved. If a child does not feel safe it will cut off access to any adult - including your own conscious adult - from entering that particular realm of decision.

To get access, you must **establish trust** with the child. You do this by bringing in someone the child already trusts – the guide. Use this to get access to hidden decisions, to change them and change your life dramatically in minutes.

Not years, not days . . . Minutes.

CHAPTER EIGHTEEN

Resolution

"Resolve, and Thou art free."
- Henry Wadsworth Longfellow

The fourth and final phase of the *Logical Soul®* process is **Resolution.** Time needed: about **5 minutes.**

Resolution takes place once you've had the **interview, discovered** what affirmation or statement best affects your hidden decision, and achieved **access** to that particular decision and changed it.

Once that decision is changed there's a process whereby you must *integrate it back into the body* - into the nervous system – for it to become permanent. Until that happens it's all a mental or emotional exercise. It remains out there in *the ethers* somewhere.

So it's important to actually solidify the new decision and anchor it into the body using a very simple method.

The Logical Soul®

Grounding Exercise

Grounding involves a short visualization, i.e., drawing energy from above into the top of the head, and pulling up energy from the center of the earth through the bottom of the feet (while either sitting or standing). You then have these energies meet in the area of the heart and the solar plexus to create a vortex of light that spreads throughout the tissues, cells, and organs of your body.

This in turn establishes the imagery of the new decision *in the body.* By doing this brief exercise, you create a powerful attraction between the new decision and the cells in your body, anchoring you into that affirmation, that new decision.

That's the simple version. You may also guide the child through a gate or some kind of portal. This is a very strong image that establishes a transition in the mind and body. Sometimes I use a very large elaborate gate on a rainbow path and the gate opens and there's a light on the other side.

I take the hand of the child and walk through this gate. On the other side - as soon as he steps over the threshold – awaits the new decision. Once you and the child step over the threshold, that new decision becomes established. It becomes emotionally real, and therefore physically real.

To wind up the visualization, you bring the child back into your heart, go back to an image of the earth, then back to your body. Come back in the body, bring in the light, and connect the whole thing.

Re-Testing

Once the re-grounding visualization is done, the changes have been made. However, in order for your **conscious mind** to accept it, a **re-test for the same affirmations** is required to show that a change actually took place. Once you see the muscle testing strong where it previously tested weak, your mind accepts this powerful demonstration to justify the inner logic of the whole process.

Resolution allows your new decision to become a physiological reality - no longer a faint idea floating out there. The *Ku* or *Unihipili* has what it needs: new support and guidance from the *Uhane* (conscious mind).

Here is a summary of the Resolution phase:

> ➢ Request a new (i.e., different) decision be made,
> ➢ Add the *"mana"* (emotional charge) through the use of guided visualization, then
> ➢ Direct the *Ku* to connect with the *Aumakua* (High Self) to create *a new prime directive!*

<u>*The importance of this phase cannot be overemphasized.*</u> Without resolution there is no new decision, no acceptance, and no change.

The *Real* Law of Attraction

By integrating this new decision into the body, your power returns. You then have the ability to put yourself out into the world and attract those things you love.

Real success, based on the Law of Attraction, does not come through need, desire, fear, or by repeating affirmations over and over. It is based on *a deep fulfillment* . . . a *knowingness* that we ARE going to get what we set out to get! And that knowingness is one of the most powerful feelings in the world.

By letting go of old prime directives, creating new ones, and anchoring them into the body, you generate the innate power to have and do anything you choose. The new inner decisions and directives will free you from the old programming that's been with you your whole life.

This is the **real** Law of Attraction . . . and the *true* meaning of success!

A Final Note on the Process

The *Logical Soul*® Process is designed to be a precise *transformational technique* that changes hidden decisions; **not** a therapy session that allows a person's *feelings* to predominate. The truth is, however, that until your partners or clients are educated, they won't understand this, and will treat the whole thing as a therapy session.

And therapy is seen to take time – often LOTS of time. In the beginning, for example, clients would talk so much I would easily spend *2 hours* trying to get them through the phases, but found it wasn't necessary. Hidden decisions – once switched – can change a person in 20 minutes as effectively as in 2 hours!

Armed with the information in this book (and hopefully some hands-on experience) you don't need to repeat my trials and errors. Just go through the process step-by-step. In the beginning at least, don't worry about spending too much time. As you get better at taking control of the process, time will fly by!

CHAPTER NINETEEN

Using the Logical Soul® for Effective Goal-Setting

"See the job. Do the job. Stay out of misery."
- Maharishi Mahesh Yogi

Can't. Never Could.

You set a goal. You work on it. You accomplish it. Easy, right?

For some people i.e., the *Great Ones* (or potential *Great Ones*) with the *Seed of Success (SOS)* ingrained in their consciousness, it *is* easy. These people can size up a situation in minutes, draw from their inner knowing and strength, gather help and resources for strengths they lack, and forge ahead to completion of a goal.

For the majority of us who carry the *Seed of Failure (SOF)* with us on a daily basis, however, achieving our goals with any degree of regularity is a very difficult task. For SOF folks there are constant pitfalls along the way, both internal and external.

First of all our *negative thoughts and fears* often stop us before we begin. Then there is the barrage of *inner doubts* to distract us, divert our attention and limit our strength and resources. If that doesn't stop us, there is the hail of *external forces* we've attracted into our lives through the law of attraction that become aligned against our goals and act as the sludge of "messes" we have to fight through daily.

How in the heck can *anyone* accomplish *anything* with such obstacles? Heck, most of the time we can't even get up enough steam to take action – *any* action!

You Are Not Alone

Judging by the sheer volume of success/motivation/affirmation programs and courses available, there are a LOT of people who have **SOF syndrome.** If your success rate for accomplishing goals is less than 85%, you are one of us.

While this may appear to be the bad news, the *good* news (?) is that most of humanity considers this "normal." The vast majority of people seldom even accomplish *half* of what they set out to do, much less complete things with any sort of regularity. So if you have *SOF Syndrome,* you have plenty of company.

Being part of the herd, however, never excited me. I'm sure it doesn't excite you either. But stats are stats, and we remain part of this large bell-curve majority of mediocre performers – that is, until a major shift happens in our lives to wake us up!

This book can be that wake up call.

The Test of Time

While the *Logical Soul®* technique is great for getting congruent inside for starting and achieving goals, how do you measure the *effectiveness* of your goal-setting program? And how do you set **benchmarks** along the way?

Single *Logical Soul®* sessions are great. Having done single sessions for over 18 years, I've found them to be very powerful, very potent; and that afterwards people reported feeling transformed.

Check out the video testimonials and case studies on our website at **www.logicalsoul.com** to get a sense of the transformations that actually took place with folks. Each session led to some transformation that molded and strengthened my clients' attitudes and inner resolve.

What happened over time, however, was not as dramatic. While the sessions were powerful I noticed that *something* began to wear off. I started re-testing people to see if their muscles were "holding" for the affirmations and results we got before. Yes, they were in most cases.

What then, I wondered, was the difficulty? Why were they again blocked? In my mind this was unacceptable, and I sought answers.

What I discovered was that while the *new decisions* they integrated inside were still intact, the **long-term habits** of how they respond to life was still ingrained by a system of **redundancy** in the subconscious mind! There were layers of *stuff* that were involved. Because the brain and mind are so complex, I actually expected this to be the case but didn't want to necessarily believe this applied to everyone.

But redundancy was there. Just as a space shuttle has a back-up for every system, there are *backup systems for our mind* and nervous system, usually put into place when we made early emotion-based decisions as a child or infant.

I noticed that although my subjects *felt* better inside, the results were still not apparent. Neural or **nerve facilitation** had set in and locked the body into a pattern of redundant responses and behaviors that did not support the new decisions.

An example of nerve facilitation would be a musician who practices a piece on the piano for several months. After enough repetitions of the same piece, it becomes automatic. The conscious mind is no longer involved, and he could possibly play this piece in his sleep! The more nerve signals pass along a nerve tissue, the easier it becomes for that nerve tissue to reach a **threshold** and fire. After a while, this firing happens faster and faster.

Similarly, unsuccessful habits build up over time. After a lifetime of unprofitable responses and behaviors, it is unlikely these will be reversed in a single session. The nervous system somehow has to be re-trained to deliver the new messages to and from the body and brain!

Patterns Can Change

Unsuccessful behaviors CAN be changed, but it takes time. How *much* time depends on the intensity of the original programming.

If you had hurt your leg and developed a limp as a child, for example, you will walk with a limp even after the cause of the limp has been healed or removed. Your body, through facilitation, had adapted to that condition. Over time (and with sufficient chiropractic care or physiotherapy), you'll start limping a little less, then a *lot* less. After a while, the limp will disappear. It just doesn't happen overnight.

Like that, when we change or transform decisions at deeper levels of our body, mind, emotions, memory and intuition, our nervous system begins to adapt to this altered condition.

Over time it will happen anyway, but if you want changes to happen faster, you must bring in new habits into your mind and physiology that compliments the changes in decision.

After *Logical Soul®* sessions, it might be a good idea to dig out some of those positive-motivation-goal-setting books, tapes, and CDs you stored in your attic years ago and forgot. They will now take on a different meaning and prove to be much more effective!

The most powerful goal-setting program I've found for me personally was Raymond Aaron's **Monthly Mentor** program. It impacted my life tremendously by giving me a way to actually *measure* my goal progress.

You can still sign up for this important training at www.monthlymentor.com.

CHAPTER TWENTY

How to Set Benchmarks for Effective Goal-Setting

"It is in your moments of decision that your destiny is shaped."
- Tony Robbins

Measuring Progress Over Time

Other than by the end results, how do you really measure your progress after setting a goal? What are your *benchmarks?*

Let's say you set a goal to achieve, say, a certain amount of money. Well, there are the obvious benchmarks you would normally set, such as whether or not you are

    a) making a certain amount today,
    b) making money next week, or

c) are you making money the week after that?

These are the benchmarks most goal-setting programs focus on. Your goal-setting mentors or teachers may also focus on your actions, i.e., certain money-making activities that you must complete each day. These are all important and part of the path to success. (And that's also why most of us with *SOF Syndrome* won't do them).

Let's assume, on the other hand, that you've cleared out much of your internal resistance (SOF) through multiple *Logical Soul®* sessions, and really feel good about your prospects for success. You can earn money, accept money, and feel worthy of getting and acting on it. What next?

The first thing to remember is that, while you have changed a hidden decision about your ability, say, to accept money, you have not really put it to the test.

So do this: **practice going out and just asking for money.** That's right; ask for a buck from a stranger. Can you do that? If not, there may still be self-worth issues related to money. This may then be something more you need to work on!

Once your worth is integrated, then **practice accepting** everything that's offered to you for a week. Can you do that? Yes? Great! If not, you might want to muscle test for accepting money on all levels and for all time.

One way of doing this is to test for *"I'm able to accept a $100,000,"* or something like that. If that's a "yes," then you will be tempted to go on to test for an amount of money *over time.* How much, for example, can you accept in two months, three months, six months? How much can you accept over a year's time? Two years? Five years?

This won't work. You must construct affirmation statements only in the **present tense.** Otherwise, your body – or *Ku* – will just tell you what it thinks you want to hear and you'll get mixed results.

You see, your low self or *Ku* does <u>not</u> understand the concept of "time." Time is abstract, i.e., from the realm of the conscious mind and intellect, or *Uhane*. Let's say I choose in six months to be able to accept a million dollars. If you're strong, it may or may not be accurate.

This is because *"six months from now"* doesn't compute. To the subconscious mind or *Ku,* there is only *"now."* So if you want to have a million dollars in six months just integrate yourself for having a million dollars, *period.* Then integrate your self for all the actions necessary to get there. Then in six months it will be there, assuming you take all the steps necessary to be in alignment with all those statements, including the one to TAKE ACTION.

I therefore express *every affirmation* in the **present tense.** While you might add *"for all time"* to any given affirmation or statement, it's really not necessary. You might also simply test daily for accepting, just to make sure it is locked in.

There is only "now" to your body, nervous system, and even the memory. Once integrated, these new inner money decisions will support your conscious goals much more powerfully . . . no matter if its now, or six years from now.

How to Set Earning Benchmarks

You are now ready to practice *earning* money. But start small. Remember, nerve facilitation works the same way in earning money as it does in learning to play a piece by Mozart. It's only a different set of activities.

Contrary to popular belief, practice does NOT make perfect. **PERFECT practice** makes perfect! Until you can get the initial steps down slowly and deliberately, you will never master the more complex world of the ultra-successful!

Again, start off with activities or goals you **know** you can accomplish. If, for example, you want to eventually earn $1,000 per day, start off with a goal to earn $100 a day first. Once you accomplish this, kick it into higher and higher gear. Just like graduating from playing *Chopsticks* to *Eine Kleine Nachtmusik,* you develop greater and greater skills with each small victory.

You are also less likely to procrastinate by choosing smaller tasks. Procrastination is just the body's way of saying *"I'm not ready for this yet,"* or *"I don't like this."* By creating a new inner decision AND creating small steps to develop new nerve pathways in the body, a new habit will be formed.

> (**Remember:** *you have spent your whole life living with the SOF telling you everything you "need" to know. Once you integrate for success instead, failure thoughts come less frequently, but they will*

still arise. When you recognize them for what they are and choose to ignore them, they lose power and will eventually disappear.)

Logical Soul® allows you to take action without all the inner resistance you are used to having. Actions then become merely something you choose to do, or not do.

The way to **overcome procrastination** is simply to test for each consecutive action required to further your goal. *"I choose to do this to further my goal." "I choose to do that."* Test for each major or minor step. If you are weak on any of these, you know there's a weak link – the one that will stop you because of a hidden decision that says you aren't ready.

Once these statements test strong, then step it up a notch. Substitute the term **"commit"** for "choose" and see how your body and *Ku* respond. **Your success is only as good as your word.** Once you can truly COMMIT to doing the things you *SAY* you're going to do, you truly step into unlimited personal power through the power of **integrity.**

How to Set Business Benchmarks

If you have to, say, hire three people in order to reach your business goal, say *"Hiring three people is the best thing I can do for my business."* Then test for that. Or *"I choose* (commit) *to hire three people to further my business."* Test for that.

If any of the statements are weak, there may be something inside of you doesn't like working with people. So if you make the statement *"I choose to hire three people"* you'll go weak every time, whether or not it's good for the business. What you're really saying is *"I hate having employees"* or *"I hate working with people."* What to do?

If you have a mentor or coach for your business (and I highly recommend you get one), they might  **show** you how to do the right things, might **tell** you what to do like hiring an employee or setting up your system, but *they can't **make** you strong inside.* That's *your* job using the *Logical Soul®*.

What a coach (or mastermind group) *can* do, however, is give you valuable *outer feedback* to know when the *inner feedback* you're getting (i.e., thoughts and feelings) is based on positive intuition, or negative fears and prejudices. If it is the latter, you must make some inner changes in order to be successful.

But maybe inner changes are NOT required! Some inner feedback is based on **intuition** - knowledge of your own deep personal makeup - and should <u>not</u> be ignored. In this case, **follow your own path!**

I know, for example, that I don't like having employees. Its not that I have a particular aversion to employees – I've had them before – it's just that I like to keep my business small. I therefore choose to outsource much of my business needs in order to do this. Intuitively, I feel this is the right path for me at this time.

And this is always your choice, but its best to know how to distinguish between *intuition* and *fear.* This is where a *mentor* or coach is invaluable. They know your business and can help guide you along the best path towards your success. Listen to them and integrate inside to reduce your fear and resistance. *Once fear is not an issue* then you can listen to your intuition and be right most of the time.

By following this plan, you are sure to succeed. It's almost foolproof. The whole thing is practical, powerful, and quick. Also, there is no need to waste a lot of money on research and development unless you are in that field already.

Simply <u>*get congruent.*</u> Establish the feeling and understanding that a particular action plan is right for you. Your subconscious (intuition) will tell you if something is right or not. Listen to this voice.

So take the time to sit down right now and test for inner decisions that may or may not be resisting your path to success. Test all the needed activities involved. You will find that by doing this, a seamless flow is established between inception of a project to its completion; from goal to action, to achievement, to fulfillment.

By listening to your body, by listening to the inner and outer benchmarks you establish every step along the way, you will come to the right decision and the right action to take each time.

CHAPTER TWENTY-ONE

The Wall

"Either this wallpaper goes, or I do!"
- Oscar Wilde, on his deathbed

Your Private Heartbreak Hill

Marathon runners know all about the Wall. *Heartbreak Hill* comes about 20 miles after the start of the Boston Marathon. It's also where the bodies of most runners become depleted of glycogen and they start hyperventilating, hallucinating, and worse.

At this point most unseasoned runners simply quit. For those who get beyond it, however, the Wall gives birth to the phenomenon of the **second wind** and they cruise to the finish line.

In the field of psychology, doctors and therapists also report hitting a wall when working with patients. This is the point where they say the patient's resistance becomes too strong to continue further with a particular session or approach. It is a point beyond the patient's paradigm, or ability to accept rational input.

Because they are highly skilled, doctors and therapists usually find a way to overcome this little problem. Sometimes they prescribe useful drugs that assist in getting past the Wall. Most often, however, they accomplish their results through means like *empathic listening,* occasional *hypnosis, a combination of drugs and listening*, and simple *persistence* over a period of time.

This usually works. With time, most people will relax with a doctor or therapist and divulge things they would *never* tell their neighbors, friends, family, or even their spouse. Time also allows the subconscious mind – with proper guidance - to eventually reveal its hidden secrets.

Author's Note: *The definitions given in this book are mostly my own. I am not a psychologist, psychiatrist; medical doctor nor philosopher, nor do I claim to cure disease or mental illness. The stories in this book are designed to illustrate my direct personal and clinical experiences only, and should not be undertaken by anyone under the direct supervision of* a medical doctor or therapist without their knowledge and consent.

In the practice of goal-setting, the same problem arises. Although obviously not severe enough to be categorized as a medical or psychiatric problem, "the Wall" in a normal person can still interfere with his or her growth, development and pursuit of happiness. Under these circumstances, it appears as a kind of low-grade and static emotional "fever" – **a feeling of being overwhelmed** - that saps the strength from our life and leaves us feeling empty inside.

From early childhood, for example, you may have been instructed to *"grow up," "be strong," "be responsible"* and *"don't trust strangers."* In the mind of a child, this translates into an initial conscious decision that later becomes a hidden one.

This may include such inner commands as *"shut down," "be stubborn," "protect what's yours"* and *"don't look at any alternatives."*

In the mind of your "inner child," the best **anchor** for this decision is *the reality at hand.* If you are talking with a person of a different race or religion but were told to never talk to strangers, you might translate that bit of information into *"don't trust Chinese people"* or Jews, or Catholics, or Hispanics, etc.

My father often criticized my childhood actions and judgments. The decision I made that *"he is smarter than me"* became a hidden decision that continued long after his death. While he is no longer around, for years I still felt inferior to others who simply *reminded* me of him.

Hidden decisions that become our prime directives each make up a brick in this "wall." I would thus define **The Wall** as follows:

*A compilation of strong emotions
And hidden decisions that define
our concept of "self."*

The Wall is there for a reason – **a very <u>good</u> reason.** In the child's mind it is the essence of who "I am." It stands as the "self" – a being separate from the rest of the world. Without this wall, you have been conditioned to feel threatened with **annihilation.** Absolute nothingness!

Therefore, any attempts your adult mind makes to breach this wall are countered by the most extreme defensive measures by your inner child who still stands guard. He or she may even resort to keep this wall by lying, cheating, stealing, or even killing.

The Wall protects you from what lies beyond it – the un-named foe described in a 1980's children's movie *The Everlasting Story* as "the Nothing." In the movie the *Nothing* sweeps through like a vortex, gobbling up everything in its path. And that's your deepest fear, i.e., looking into the Abyss. Annihilation. The Wall, despite its restrictions, appears to protect you from this horrible fate.

Overcoming Your Private Fairy Tale

This Wall cannot protect you, however. It never could, actually, since it is really made up of a *host of stories* and created by a *lie*. It is a useless mental/emotional "thing" that stands in the middle of your life and holds you back from proceeding ahead in EVERY direction you wish to move. And don't forget – the Wall protects *nothing!*

There is literally nothing behind the Wall - the only threat is to your imaginary "self." You simply cannot look at this void, or else you feel the world as you know it would crumble to dust.

That's also why **the Wall will never, ever disappear**. It will remain as long as you do.

While it can't be removed, it can be temporarily *transcended* to allow *hidden decisions* to rise to the surface and fall away! The first time this happened to me was in 1992 . . .

More About Cathy

I first discussed the discovery of the Wall in my initial work with Cathy in Chapter 7.

From the beginning of this meeting with her I felt there was a faint but noticeable resistance in the air I couldn't quite put my finger on. I said something to Cathy about getting clear about our business objectives before we proceeded, and she also thought it was a good idea. I figured that unless we did this, the business would fail and we couldn't make money working together.

As a chiropractor I had worked with lots of patients clearing mental and emotional blocks to their health and well-being. As I still do today, I had them make a statement while using *AK* (applied kinesiology) to test the strength or weakness of their underlying beliefs.

Unlike the *Logical Soul®* method today, however, I had no way then of finding the CAUSE of most of these blocks. I figured that my intent to release them was good enough. With this in mind I set out to find the cause of the resistance, and release all inner blocks between us.

Then came *the Wall*, the point I'd run across many times before where my releasing therapy could not penetrate. It had happened with others and was happening again this time.

I had Cathy make a statement and she tested weak. I don't remember what the statement was, but it had something to do with the ability to accept something. Whatever it was, the issue was blocked and could *not* be released, no matter what I tried.

The thought came to see if access was available to change that particular program. Yes it was. I then asked

"Is access available to me?" No.
"To Cathy?" It was no also. I was suddenly halted again.

This final dilemma had me stumped. I didn't know what to do. I had come to the point to where access was available, but it was not available to me, *or even Cathy,* at least not consciously.

I stopped for a moment and sat there saying nothing. I remember at the time of having the thought "what happens if you ask *the wall* what it needs in order to allow us to get through..."

I began to muscle test and asked Cathy's *Ku* different questions. The questions had to do with certain decisions that were made in her past that led to this closed loop, this Wall. It was like talking to a child – in fact Cathy's inner child – that no longer trusted adults. Since Cathy and I were both adults, this lack of feedback from inside was a delicate issue.

To make a long story short, I was able to get access beyond the Wall for a very short time – enough to awaken some hidden force that caused quite a stir. It took a couple of days – and a threat from her boyfriend - to get the answers I needed to calm the churning waters of emotion and fear.

I was finally able to get Cathy stable. Afterwards, she reported feeling better than she had in a long time, and that issue tested strong for her thereafter.

I had discovered the *Key to SAFE Access*: **Personal Archetypes.** These vary from person to person, and must be found individually. Since no person has the same history, for example, as Cathy's, no one has the same archetypes with her, i.e., a trusted person, pet or thing from her childhood or past that allows the access beyond *the Wall.* This approach makes it both safe and effective.

By invoking the name and presence of this being at critical times, there is a rapid inward process that takes place – a transcending – beyond the Wall. With the conscious mind fully present, a **new decision** is put in place of the old or destructive one, creating a **new prime directive** for the *Ku.*

Although we never went into business together, Cathy and I shared this knowledge ever since. So far as I know she has since gone beyond her fears and come into a space of complete inner-acceptance.

The Un-Therapy

One thing I discovered after working with Cathy and others was that **the *Logical Soul*® is *not* about therapy.** Although it can certainly be used as a tool by doctors and therapists, it was something uniquely different.

Most therapies – whether it is hypnotherapy, psychotherapy, logo-therapy, regression therapy, or even my chosen field of chiropractic – operate on the basis of **treatment,** i.e., *"something is wrong."* The therapist either attempts to give some relief to the patient, or release barriers to the person's pent-up anger, fear or other subconscious block to his or her natural human expression. The idea is that, by redirecting thoughts and energies to more positive intentions, the resulting actions will naturally lead to a well-adjusted individual.

And it usually works. Therapies – and therapists - are greatly needed. But even in this so-called enlightened age, most people still shy away from admitting they "need" therapy . . . particularly men. Rightly or wrongly, many believe that therapy is a long term commitment, and they are neither sick enough nor wealthy enough to avail themselves of these services. That means most of us are simply left to our own devices.

And that's OK, since there actually is another way. The fact is, that even if we avail ourselves of therapy and release much of our pent up anger, frustration, fears and hang-ups, <u>the decisions these emotions are based on have not changed</u>. Most of the same *stuff* will therefore return later when future stress re-creates the same circumstances as the original fear or hang-up.

The reason this happens has to do with another aspect of therapy that is usually overlooked. The very concept of "therapy" means that something is not right, or needs to be fixed. If this something involves the subconscious mind, the therapist will naturally treat the subconscious mind as a thing to be manipulated, rather than an actual being (the *Ku*) with whom to communicate.

This simple **lack of respect** for our inner being cuts us off from results that would otherwise come to us. I mean, how would YOU feel if you were treated like a "thing"? Personally, I would be a little miffed.

But therapy certainly has its place, and I'm certainly not opposed to it. Quite the contrary, I refer people to therapists all the time and feel it can do wonders for patients and clients who need the attention for deep-seated fears, phobias or addictions.

In fact, I will insist on someone seeing a therapist if they report feeling unstable. In fact, I am considering a program to train doctors and therapists in using the *Logical Soul®* in their practice to increase their overall effectiveness.

The *Logical Soul®* is not about curing fears and phobias, although these will usually disappear as part of the procedure. It's about **transformation.** This process is about taking you from the ordinary realm of existence to the extra-ordinary. It's about taking you *beyond the Wall* in an instant *without* stirring up a bunch of emotional drama and painful memories and fears.

This kind of transformation allows you to break out of your boundaries and soar; create miracles in your life, and move into a life free of the problems that plague you.

TAKE A MOMENT RIGHT NOW to check out the last chapter of this book for a special offer. Then ACT on it. You won't be sorry.

CHAPTER TWENTY-TWO

The Strange Case of Free Will

"You must believe in free will. There is no choice."
- Isaac B. Singer (1904-1991)

The Great Debate

Do we really have this thing called *free will?* Or are we destined to live out our days following a pattern set out for us by our genetic makeup and early childhood impressions?

Yes, I know. This is the riddle freshmen Psychology and Philosophy students debate endlessly after some professor hits them with it for the first time.

It's also a question that has no simple answer.

Consequently we lose interest as we grow older, opting instead to focus on more practical inquiries such as *"how much money can I bring home this month?"* Somehow, I believe there IS a simple answer... but I'll come to that later.

Because of its importance, the debate over *Free Will vs. Determinism* has been going on ever since Darwin and Freud started shaking up our ideas about human life and consciousness. It's also a field where no one really knows, but everyone has an opinion. So here's mine . . .

In one corner live the **Free Will Advocates** – those bubbling Optimists who champion the idea that everything is possible for those who persist and think happy thoughts. Freedom is the most important ingredient in their lives and in the society they would hope to inhabit. Their world operates on this basic idea: free markets, free thought, free speech, and the freedom to choose their lives and destinies.

In the other corner dwell the **Darlings of Determinism**, or denizens of despair. These modern Calvinists sincerely believe that all humans are controlled by some chaotic coincidence based on evolution and eons of probability and adaptation. The 18th Century version of this person was actually the optimist of his day, i.e., the curious scientist who believed that God wound up the Universal "clock" and set it running. This *Newtonian-Cartesian* principle would later be challenged in the early 20th Century by Einstein's treatises on Relativity.

The modern version of Determinism states that all behavior can be charted, predicted, and shown to be a function of Neuro-Anatomy, Chaos Theory, being jacked into the *Matrix,* or some other important-sounding principle that we should all know about but don't.

In my world – and probably the world of most people - both free will and determinism have a place. Most of us simply don't have the time or mental endurance to process this question thoroughly. So we let it exist in our lives as an unsolved paradox.

I actually think that, at least in this case, laziness is wisdom. A seeming paradox is not bad . . . it simply has not found a resting place yet.

This means – for me anyway – that paradox is a major part of what we call our "reality."

Life on Cruise Control

I have "free will." I can choose to turn on the TV, leave it running. I can call a friend long distance and leave the phone on the table. I can walk this way – no that way – no I can then sit down. Or I can eat a banana, throw the peel on the floor, slip on it. Then I can get up, walk out of the door, get into my car, and drive 4,000 miles to North Saskatchewan, Canada, to watch glaciers melt.

So why don't I just do all those things?

Well, I could if I *wanted* to, but (and here's the "but") I don't *want* to!! (so there!!)

The fact is I DON'T have free will <u>until I can completely understand – and transcend – all the "buts" in my life.</u>

"But Michael" (more "buts") *"That's crazy! Why would I want to do things that make no logical sense??"*

Good question. Here's my answer:

Logic manifests in our every thought and action. Childhood observations tend to become *inner logic,* instinct or early programming, whereas adult understanding is generally considered the more "real" or "outer" logic. This is so, simply by virtue of the fact that we all have been indoctrinated time and again by family, social and cultural norms, etc.

Outer logic is that part of us who considers leaving on the TV and phone is wasteful (it is). **Inner logic,** on the other hand, involves the feelings, memories and impressions involved with such a decision – those factors lying within the realm of the Low Self or *Ku.* Does going away and leaving the TV on invoke a feeling of power as a form of rebellion against a strict father? If so, that inner logic will override so-called common sense and prompt you to rebel.

Logic acts as our Cruise control. Both inner and outer logic steer our ship (mind, body and ego) through life with the minimum of loss, discomfort and pain. But there is a trade-off. If all "selves" are in alignment, we will act according to what is referred to as common sense. If they are misaligned, however, the outcome is self-sabotage . . . the result of conflicting forces battling one another.

When such battles occur, the so-called "you" that comprises both forces cannot win:

> **When the conscious mind (*Kane*) abdicates control and the *Ku* takes over,** the inner logic often leads us into drama, addiction, rage, terror, sickness, or just plain

chaos. The *Ku* runs on feelings without the guidance of its "big brother *Kane*" to smoothe out the bumps along the way.

Conversely, when the *Ku* abandons the conscious mind, this results in the person shutting down the factory, so to speak. All the workers have gone home, except for those keeping the basic functions running! The result is that of shock; symptoms include feeling blank, depressed, shut down, surreal and detached. *Victims of disasters,* i.e., earthquakes, hurricanes, tsunamis, etc., often exhibit these symptoms. Usually they are short-lived, but may also last for many years.

So which is it: do we have Free Will or Determinism? I believe *both* are present, but determinism usually holds most of the cards. Free will comes in *only* during the decision to

1) act consciously and
2) maintain the alignment between *Ku* and *Kane*.

The Inevitable Mr. Hyde

Do we even have the free will to determine our own *dreams* and *aspirations?* Or do these dreams create the basis of determinism for how we live our lives?

Have you ever wondered what it would be like to wake up one morning in the body of a *monster?* Ugly face, skin, eyes, hair, lips, nose and other features? What would you do if you suddenly had the urge to run around smashing things or raping someone?

Scary, isn't it...

This happened one night to an English writer during a dream in 1885. He awoke screaming and instantly set about writing his masterpiece *Dr. Jekyll and Mr. Hyde,* the tale of a doctor suddenly transformed into a raging beast.

Robert Louis Stevenson's book was an overnight success, primarily because his strait-laced Victorian audience immediately understood the power of the beast within each one of them – a beast that could at any moment be unleashed on an unsuspecting public.

Stephenson and other authors, like Mary Shelley (*Frankenstein*) and Bram Stoker (*Dracula*), found an unexplored Victorian niche – fear of the inner beast – and were able to capture the hearts and imaginations of their audience because of the universal nature of this phenomenon.

While we no longer live in a society bound by Victorian morals, monster characters who represent the *"inner beast"* remain popular. Our *real* inner beast – the *Ku* – is still urging us to let go and follow the wild. Exotic vacations, wild parties, rock concerts and the ever-growing presence of horror and porno movies allow us a chance to "let it all hang out" and still be considered safe and sane.

The point is, we all have inner urges that drive us – our thoughts, fears, feelings, and wants. These are, for the most part, the seeds of our failure or success in life.

Do you want success? Connect with the hidden logic of *your* "Mr. Hyde" to attract wealth, health, love and happiness!

CHAPTER TWENTY-THREE

Our Inner Default Settings

"The basis of Optimism is sheer terror."
- Oscar Wilde

Sometimes That's All There Is

I've spent the preceding chapters establishing how we are run by hidden decisions that are, in fact, accessible and changeable. Now the bad news: some people are simply run by pre-determined factors and **not all inner hidden decisions are changeable.** Some of these decisions are really stuck in our genes – tissues, cells and organs - and won't disappear no matter how many times we access and attempt to change them.

Most of the people who harbor such non-changeable hidden decisions appear to be mostly normal and functional. They are seen as a bit quirky, but are nonetheless accepted as one of us.

The non-changing aspect of these hidden decisions, however, powerfully asserts itself in ways that are neither pleasant nor "normal." Yet the vast majority of the people I speak of cannot be classified as mentally ill. They are the *"walking wounded"* or those harboring a sub-clinical affliction, addiction, or neurosis.

One example is an adult client of mine – I'll call him "Gilbert" – who came to me wanting to deal with his severe inability to attract money. He came across as supremely confident, and was almost always optimistic about the success that lay just around the corner for him.

This was, however, in noticeable contrast to his demeanor. Despite his outer confidence (and braggadocio), Gilbert came across as a bit wild-eyed, slovenly, and often scattered.

One of the first things I discovered about Gilbert was that he was given up for adoption as an infant. While this of itself might seem to be un-remarkable, all of Gilbert's life issues appeared to be connected to **one fundamental issue:** the **terror** of separation from his birth mother at such a young age, and the most basic – I call it organic - **decision** to squelch self-reflection in order to help him survive this trauma.

Predictably, Gilbert's secondary hidden decisions revolved around safety, love, belonging and intimacy. He never had a long-term relationship, always felt a need to assert himself around others, exhibited noticeable ADHD, and was unable to relax. Muscle testing revealed he did not feel safe, would never feel safe, and must constantly be in action in order to survive.

I held countless *Logical Soul®* sessions with Gilbert – asking all the right questions, accessing and changing hidden decisions and even accessing the decisions of his birth parents and ancestors (see more on this topic in **Chapter 25**). None of it had any long-term effect. There were a few moments when his humanity shone through, these were but fleeting episodes and disappeared rapidly with the slightest distraction.

What I came to realize with Gilbert simply was what he was. Regardless of what I considered "healthy" in an individual life, Gilbert had his own internal logic that would never relinquish its dominance. *He was built to survive, and survive he did.*

Gilbert could never allow himself to get *beyond* the survival paradigm, since taking *that* step had no basis in his reality. There was simply no nerve circuitry that would allow it.

Organic Decisions

Although we were able to positively change Gilbert's money situation a little, complete transformation has been elusive. The uncertainty instilled in his mind and nervous system at such a young age arose from an interruption in the normal maturing process of an infant – something called *separation-individuation.* Because of the trauma of becoming separated from his mother before he was a month or two old, Gilbert never bonded with his birth mother and missed a crucial stage in his development. [22]

The same thing, by the way, can happen to a person whose parent is very controlling or inflicts "smother love" at an early age. The person as a young child never had a chance to develop what might be considered his or her normal survival skills. The parent had pre-empted any such individual will and stunted their development.

I remember embryology classes in Chiropractic College that talked about the crucial stages of fetal development in the womb, and how interference with any of those stages could lead to malformation, stunted growth or dysfunction.

The fact is, **we didn't stop developing after leaving the womb.** It is arguably true that the whole journey from fertilized egg to adulthood is one where *anything* can go wrong – and something almost always does. If its not cleft palate, it is phobias about spiders, heights, performance or intimacy.

We ALL have *stuff* to deal with. That's just the way it is. Some stuff, however, is easier to access and change than other stuff.

I've found over the years that the *Logical Soul®* works very well for those clients whose childhood was relatively normal and supportive, at least until age 3 or so. Non-verbal "decisions" that result from trauma prior to this age tend to be well-established and stubbornly resist any attempts to even locate them.

Verbal (thinking) skills and cognitive abilities are lacking in a toddler before he or she can speak.

Consequently, decisions made at such a young age are similar to those made by a fetus . . . or an *amoeba* for that matter. Such decisions are *non-verbal* and based simply on the same nerve firings found in an elemental organism that seeks to avoid pain and find pleasure.

These **"organic decisions"** arise out of the very first level of *Maslow's Hierarchy of Needs.* They will not change until they are fulfilled. And, because the infant has not yet developed the ability to separate him or herself from the environment, fulfillment cannot come from the outside. Feedback is difficult if not impossible to introduce, **ergo: no change is possible from the outside.**

The Solution

While I cannot "heal" such an organic-decision-bound person, I can surround him or her with an aura of love, caring and empathy that will speak to the isolated *Ku* inside. Many people in such isolation are akin to an *autistic child* – at least with regards to their unchanging organic decisions.

While I would never diagnose them as such, I've observed that the organic-decision-bound individual has many similarities to someone bound by autism. There is a shutting-off of anything that would interfere with the inner prime directive.
It may be helpful to look at autism, if only to find a possible solution. There have been several instances where autistic children were brought back from a world of continued isolation by parents who refused to give up on them. Like that, I believe there is hope for the isolated adult as well.

The problem with us grown-ups, however, is that so much is expected of us. When we reach the age where we are considered mature, we are no longer considered cute, cuddly or adorable. Baby talk is frowned upon and we are expected to earn a living, perform, and be responsible for others.

Authenticity is lost as we struggle to adapt to grown-up expectations and rapidly-changing environmental pressures. For those who appear to remain lost or scattered, we label them as having been touched by *schizophrenia, Asperger's Syndrome, substance addict, severe ADHD, obsessive-compulsive disorder (OCD),* or any of a myriad range of disorders. As in the days of the ancient Shamans, we figure that by giving their problem a label, we can control them . . . or at least know a way to deal with them when we must.

For a person whose life is run by organic decisions, the only answer is the presence of both **grace** and **love.**

Grace and Love

Love is the complete acceptance of what is. **Grace** is response of the High Self to purposeful Love with Intent. *Together, Grace and Love can overcome any obstacle, solve any problem, and heal any disease or affliction* . . . even that of the sub-clinical, but organic-decision-bound individual. Both grace and love come together to form finer and finer levels of **consciousness** until pure (or God) Consciousness is achieved – this being the stated (or unstated) goal of every religion.

Grace and love can also come together in very practical ways – ways in which people come together and share a bond that invokes a divine presence. A great example of how this works is *Alcoholics Anonymous (AA)* and similar twelve-step programs. Human beings with pre-verbal (organic) decisions binding them have few places to find complete acceptance, companionship, and a guided opportunity for grace. AA and similar groups provide that.

The fact that the founder – known simply as "Bill" – was able to rise from the depths of his own addiction and fifty years later powerfully touch the life of my Father-in-law in Germany during the last years of his life, speaks volumes to the ever-expansive power of Grace.

There is an old saying: *"When the disciple is ready, the master will appear."* What does it take to be ready? Simply approach the master. In the very first chapter of the Hindu holy book - the **Bhagavad-Gita -** Arjuna (the disciple) approaches Lord Krishna (the master). The whole story of enlightenment arises out of Krishna's teachings to Arjuna.

Had Krishna made the first move towards Arjuna, nothing would have happened. The disciple – only by taking the first action with Intent – affirms his or her readiness. Asking a doctor or partner to work with you creates a similar dynamic.

Similarly, by proclaiming yourself a "sinner" and accepting Jesus Christ as your personal savior, your sins are supposedly washed away. Those who have undergone *salvation* report a feeling of deep contentment that stays with them always. Those who seek *Sartori* in the teachings of Gautama Buddha also report a rising inner contentment.

For the organic-decision-bound person, action is also required before any relief can be obtained. No one – not family, friends, loved ones, nor any master himself – can bring relief to this person. The desire to seek help *must arise from somewhere deep within the individual.*

My personal awakening was from an opening of awareness <u>not</u> associated with any person or deity. I therefore had trouble accepting "personal salvation" although I remained firmly *spiritual* in my longing.

Whether or not the spiritual yearning is **personal** or **impersonal,** the **desire itself** is the only opening that Grace requires.

Forms of Grace

Grace can arrive through many forms. To a Christian it is through *Jesus.* To a Hindu, *Brahma, Vishnu, Shiva* or one of any number of *Avatars* reveals the path. *Mohammed* guides the Muslim, and bowing down to a statue of *the Buddha* can be seen on practically every corner in Nepal, Thailand and Sri Lanka.

True Grace, however, is formless. It is tasteless, colorless, featureless, and timeless. While organized religions around the world seek to capture grace in the form of a savior, master, guru, or saint; and search for it in their scriptures, temples, holy places, and sacred rites or relics, *true Grace remains elusive.*

True Grace is never born and will never die. It cannot be sought, nor can it be held or contained when it arrives. It is the tempest without the wind, heat without the sun, and majesty without the gorgeous scenery. It is the holy within the temple, but also outside of it. It can be felt in all of these places and things . . . and in other ways that may seem unimaginable.

When I stared into the eyes of a dying infant in Sri Lanka, and held my mother's hand as she took her final breath, I felt the presence of Grace stronger than at any other moments in my life. The form was totally unexpected and the presence, unmistakable.

Grace is a form of personalized consciousness - the substance that makes up our reality. Never-changing by itself, it shall always remain . . . ever-changing.

Changeable Defaults

Through Grace, the non-changeable _can_ change. Since Grace can never be harnessed, however, how can change happen?? Let's look at another example:

Let's say I want to build a sacred temple to honor God. How do I invite Grace to enter?

The first thing I would think to do is build the temple with tender, loving care. The more care that goes into it (I reason), the more Grace is possible – not because it is "earned" but because of the desire to accept it when it arrives, and the increased feeling of "deserving" that allows me to accept it when it does show up. My reasoning is: if I make Grace feel at home, she will come.

That may be true or not. I know many VERY elaborate temples that took years and decades to build, and became sacred monuments to the deity they were meant to honor. In so participating in this sacred process, the devotees becomes blessed or awakened.

But this is a whole subject in and of itself. In the next chapter, we explore the realm of meaning, ritual, and consciousness.

CHAPTER TWENTY-FOUR

Ritual & Taboo: A Conspiracy of Meaning

"He who has a 'why' to live can bear with almost any 'how.'"
- Friedrich Nietzsche

Those Things We Do...

A **ritual** is defined as any repetitive activity that is perceived by the actor as meaningful or important. Rituals attempt to invoke a hidden force or power perceived to be spiritual or religious, even if the person is not consciously engaging these meanings.

The ritual is also used to cancel out, or lessen the effect of invoking or acting according to a **taboo,** or forbidden action. This ritual-taboo dance has its roots in tribal cultures, where strict adherence to the former and avoidance of the latter is, for them, a matter of life and death.

Eating is normally considered to be a necessary part of living, i.e., a habit. Jesus, however, brought a different meaning into the act, and his *Last Supper* has become the center of ritual wine and wafer offerings in the Christian church for almost two thousand years. This ritual helps offset the weekly sins we have committed or taboos we have invoked during that period, and it supposedly cleanses us, at least until the following week when we must do it all again.

A more mundane example of a ritual might be the act of brushing the hair of a loved one who is terminally ill or just passed away. Or it could take the form of simply brushing your teeth after the loss of a job or career. Events that happen just after a major event in one's life become memorable.

I will never forget where I was and what I was doing when I learned JFK was shot, the Apollo 11 astronauts landed on the moon, and the morning of September 11, 2001. These sudden events took on a huge significance for me, personally, and for the society as a whole.

In the cases I just described, the *meaning* came first, then attached itself to the action. Watching TV is not a ritual in my house. Watching jets crash into the World Trade Center, however, gave this activity a *meaning* during that moment in time. Either way, it suddenly became an important *ritual* at that moment in time to sit and watch replays of the event and its aftermath. Now, whenever that or similar events are repeated, the same reverent feeling occurs.

Rituals and taboos play an important part in our everyday lives because we apparently NEED them to function properly and keep on living. Even seemingly unimportant rituals have a huge impact on the ones who create and use them. Some baseball players, for example, go through an entire set of routines when getting ready to hit, e.g. loosening and tightening batting gloves, kicking the toes in the dirt, tapping the bat on the plate, and rocking back and forth. A singer might practice her scales and sets only TWO times (instead of five) on the day of a performance.

In the cases of the baseball player and singer, rituals are used to enhance the meaning (success in their job) and avoid the taboo (failing their job). Me - I spilled some salt the other day, so I threw some over my right shoulder. Or was it the left...? This was obviously *a ritual I inherited* since success, failure or death were not impending issues.

Rituals take on special importance when **archetypal imagery** is invoked. And the more the better. Have you ever seen a Las Vegas gambler at work? His every move is deliberate, serious, and thoughtful. While fun is the main objective for the weekend gambler, it's serious business to the Pro, and even a matter of survival to the gambling addict.

Failure, to a life-long gambler is the fear that is present at every turn. He will therefore do *anything* to avoid it. He will blow on the dice, gather around all the "lucky" people, gyrate the same way he did when he last won, and call out to the heavens during every throw. Heck, if having a coven of witches brew a strange concoction next to the craps table actually worked, you bet your *eye of newt* he would have it!

As long as it *means* something, it can be used for good . . . or ill.

The Search for Meaning

Do rituals and taboos work? Yes *and* No. They are important in that they add meaning to our lives. That's it. Without them, life – under ordinary circumstances - still goes on. Nature, in fact, has its own "rituals," i.e., day-night, winter-summer, hot-cold, acid-alkaline, and billions of other repeating cycles that make up the fabric of life.

But while nature may have a built-in intelligence, no *thought* goes into it. My cat, for example, might have invented a ritual of crying a certain way when he wants food, but in reality, he's just crying for food. His so-called "ritual" is actually my perception. While crying for food is definitely a habit, I suspect *Mr. Pookey* doesn't really care. If I don't feed him, he will go into his next phase – biting my ankles until I scream for mercy and open the can.

In the same way as animals are driven by instinct and training, so too are most humans. Is putting on your socks, brushing your teeth and driving your car to work a ritual? Probably not, unless you are going to your wedding, divorce or death.

Short of impending death or major life changes, habits are not what I consider "rituals" although they could be. They are instinctive acts based on earlier training and repetition.

Rituals come into play most dramatically in times of survival. During such times or events, each act becomes meaningful or we die.

Victor Frankl in his treatise *Man's Search for Meaning*[23] emphasized that during his internment at the Dachau concentration camp in Germany, he found it imperative to add a special meaning to everything, especially suffering. By surviving the war, he reasoned he would be able to identify his tormentors afterwards and could answer to his God and deceased family members.

Revenge became the context for everything he did; his major tool for survival. All subsequent survival actions became an ongoing ritual, a sacred duty to those he promised he would survive. And he did.

Frankl's greatest contribution after the war was the creation of the "Third Viennese School of Psychotherapy" or **Logotherapy.** It is a type of existentialist analysis that focuses on a *will to meaning* as opposed to Adler's Nietzschean doctrine of **will to power** or Freud's **will to pleasure.** Rather than power or pleasure, *logotherapy* is founded upon the belief that it is the striving to find a meaning in one's life that is the primary, most powerful motivating and driving force in man.[24]

Ritual and Everyday Life

Used consciously (as in *Logotherapy*) ritual becomes, well, *meaningful!* Conscious living is indeed happier living, according to those who espouse this approach, and may be the *only* means of survival in cases of torture or very difficult times. Most religions and spiritual practices focus on some forms of ritual as integral to a long, happy and healthy life, and indeed see no other way to live.

Even Agnostics, Atheists, and strict Darwinists have their own rituals, albeit non-denominational in scope and practice. While I cannot verify Ernie Pyle's assertion that *"there are no atheists in foxholes"* I can say that meaning definitely has a place in the lives of those non-believers who believe in <u>something.</u> An atheist might still blow on the dice, for example, or avoid stepping on sidewalk cracks . . . for whatever reasons he won't tell you.

Indeed, **Memes** are rituals that have taken hold of our minds and control our actions. Whether we consciously invited them in, or inherited them from our family, teachers or ancestors, *memes* by nature will persist. In fact, that is their only goal – to persist by whatever means (and *memes*) necessary!

Organized religion is an established, socially-acceptable meme with many sets of sub-memes (rituals and taboos) that uphold its prominence.

I suspect we invent rituals and taboos because <u>we have to feel somehow that our lives matter</u>. If our life doesn't matter – and God (or "the gods" or "Spirit" or "*Chi*") are not watching – we might as well just walk over a cliff and end the whole thing, right? Some, in fact, do.

If your life is bound by memes and rituals, this belief is reality. If going to heaven as a Jihad Muslim means you have to blow yourself up in the marketplace, this ritual then IS your life. But your life will be very short, and probably none too happy.

Once you allow yourself to see through cultural and societal restrictions, however, the whole thing becomes apparent for what it is - a cultural and ego-supporting **game** – one which you can choose to play, or not.

If we CANNOT see these memes as games, however, we become pawns in the game of control by the so-called powers that be: the church, political leadership, or news media. Even Darwinists are caught up with the evolution meme and can't allow conflicting ideas to encroach onto their convictions.[25] To the uninformed, memes are the rituals that control their minds and urge them to enforce these same rituals on others.

In Sri Lanka, India and Thailand, they train elephants using a very simple technique. When the elephant is very young, they tie them to a peg stuck in the ground. Because the elephant is a baby, it does not yet have the strength to break free, and stops when it feels the restriction. As the elephant grows and ages, however, the training ritual is the same: tie the elephant using the same leg, same rope and the same peg in the ground. Consequently, even a fully-grown elephant will not be able to break free of his rope and peg.

The ritual wins. He is stuck.

Like that, we hear beliefs, dogmas, and rules from our elders, parents, teachers, preachers and Rabbis.

We spend the first half our lives *listening to others* about what is important in life.

Then we spend the latter part of our lives *convincing others* these ideas are right – our own children and those impressionable souls we wish to save. The only problem is, if those others don't agree, suddenly our life becomes meaningless and that heralded "mid-life crisis" comes out of the closet.

Like the evil Boogeyman we imagined as a child, our loss of meaning can become fatal. Living life as if *nothing* matters is self-defeating and life-denying. "Existential angst" can lead to apathy, self-sabotage, and a loss of one's center.

It can also be an opening to self-realization.

The Third Way

When I underwent a cosmic experience around age thirteen, I became aware of how utterly IN-significant human clumps of matter really are. Once I really understood that there are billions and billions of stars out there, and that each one we see in the sky is part of only ONE galaxy – the Milky Way – and that there are billions and billions of other galaxies beyond this one, billions and trillions of light years away . . . the enormity of my surroundings boggled my mind to a state of standstill that lasted for many years.[26]

For over six years, nothing mattered – my grades, friends, family, play, nothing. I went through the motions of eating, sleeping and schoolwork, but all meaning had slid into obscurity. I collected comic books as a way to at least dream of an escape as a super hero, but even this became meaningless as time went on.

My life seemed completely hopeless, yet I came out of this self-imposed exile and self-destruction after about half-dozen years by realizing there was something very real that connected all this *stuff* – the distant galaxies and my body and mind - together: **consciousness.**

****

Today my life is full, but remains uncertain. I'm caught up in neither belief nor disbelief. To me, there is a fulfilling third way . . . as one who simply lives, loves, and feels gratitude towards all events and beings. There is an acceptance of the sheer uncertainty of life – the mystery of being.

You might assert this is simply another meme that I've adopted. Maybe you're right, but I don't think so. The worldview was one I *tried* previously to adopt, but failed miserably. You see, I don't believe true happiness, contentment, or gratitude can be forced or adopted. It arises naturally from within oneself . . . once the fetters of memes, rituals, limiting beliefs, and conflicting hidden decisions have fallen away.

The *Logical Soul*® is a way to let go of this *stuff* and begin to allow the natural happiness within to come out and play. Once true freedom arises, the need for ritual drops away, as does the fear of taboos.

This does *not* mean, however, that you will start running around acting cruelly or irresponsibly. Quite the contrary, by living a happy and contented life, *you will naturally do the right thing* for yourself and others. You will start living life in accordance with the laws of nature and the Divine!

Pure consciousness is not something you *do* . . .

It's who you *are* . . . deep inside!

CHAPTER TWENTY-FIVE

Ancestral Decisions

"Traditions are the guideposts driven deep in our own subconscious minds. The most powerful ones are those we can't even describe, aren't even aware of."
- Unknown

There's a Whole Lot of Stuff In There

What is the role of **ancestors** and family in your **goal setting,** in your life? It's probably not what you think.

Ancestors play into your consciousness in ways that are deeply-ingrained for the simple reason we ARE our ancestors! We carry their DNA. Family beliefs. Traditions. More than that, we carry the cellular memory of things we could never know about consciously, even in our wildest imaginings.[27]

One example comes from an old saying that underscores this reality: *"When you marry your wife, you marry her family."* The same may be said for the other side: husbands bring family with them also, although not so obviously in many cultures. Before my wife and I can be intimate - or even have a meaningful conversation – we must clear away the *stuff* from friends and work, and also from family.

They are always with us, whether we like it or not; deny it or not. It has been known for a long time that family abuse tendencies are passed on from generation to generation. Whether or not the "sins of the father" are passed on to the fourth and fifth generations, I don't know, but apparently there is plenty of research and evidence to support it. [28]

But why do we take on this . . . *stuff?*

Ancestral Influence is Strong

There are those who argue that **free will** plays a part in all this.

"I mean, what the heck does the fact that my great-great-grandfather abused his wife, sons and daughters have to do with my current decisions to be a good citizen and loving father?"

Nothing, really. *Except* that the cellular memory of this abuse may still be there, waiting to unfold in the form of cancer, arthritis, Alzheimer's disease, or a heart attack. Since modern culture looks down on such behavior – at least in public – it hides inside. Unable to express in ways which are now considered politically or socially incorrect, a hidden decision will manifest in ways that ARE acceptable, i.e., self-inflicted wounds, diseases, or accidents.

Free will does _not_ involve our hidden decisions, primarily because we don't even know about them! So-called "Free will" therefore, if it exists at all, is _limited to the world we consciously know about_ – a very small world.

> **Author's Note:** *While I assert the idea of limited free will and the passing on of ancestral decisions, this is only a working hypothesis. This "fact" is something I use primarily as a tool to access and change hidden decisions. The results seem to support its effectiveness. Refer back to Chapters 22 and 23 for more discussion of this important topic.*

Your Roots are Close to Home

Your relationship with family and ancestors is often very subtle. It's not something you normally think about, day to day, unless your family is somehow involved in your goal setting. If you are young, you may feel your family is standing in the way. When you're older, the family becomes your responsibility.

Many cultures - Oriental for example – incorporate ancestor worship. Native Americans also had conversations with deceased relatives and with tribes of elders. Shamans conversed with these elders constantly. There are all sorts of examples in every culture that ancestors play a vital role in that culture.

Even in the west, most of our **modern rituals** are based on ancient connections with our ancestral roots in order to seek their blessings. Lighting the Christmas tree and the burning of candles and a Yule log bring to life the central European yearning for warmth and happiness in the cold dead of winter. The birth, death and resurrection of **Jesus of Nazareth,** a remake of the resurrection of the Egyptian god **Osiris,** reminds us of the eternal cycle of life and the natural death and rebirth in the Winter and Spring.

In fact, the word "religion" means "tie back" – the natural human tendency to re-populate the present with our real roots. We yearn for ties to God, the Spirit, or spirits of the past. Without the blessings of the past, we feel we are nothing; have nothing. When we deny this same past, or feel cut off from it by "sinning" (i.e., an old archery term meaning "*to miss the mark*") we feel a sort of internal chaos – a real loss.

According to the **Huna,** the only real sin is "hurting another." When this happens, the *Ku* feels ashamed and cuts off the communication with the High Self. Over time, our connections to the past begin to disappear more rapidly and we feel more and more uprooted and lost.

In the West, however, there is also a tradition of science. Letting go of the past became practically enshrined as the scientific method which replaced flawed observations by the five senses, intuition and ancestral influences. We also lost that connection with the *Ku* spoken of in **Chapter 11.** Intuition, myths and legends lost their place in a world dominated by *Newtonian-Cartesian* reasoning. Anything unable to stand up to rigid physical or logical proof was discarded.

In North America, we even took that a step further with the gradual dissolution of families. Although family still plays a part, our individual goals, aspirations and destiny takes priority. "Do your own thing" became a national obsession, a natural outgrowth of the pioneer spirit that formed the USA.

When we ignore family, we also ignore a part of ourselves that could be much more potent, much more powerful. As we acknowledge and grow within a family, we create a high touch environment where we start to see the world as we do our families. If we're disconnected from our parents then we're disconnected - at least in part - from the world.

So, like it or not, we still seek our parents' blessings and approval whether they are alive or dead. *We seek it whether stated or unstated.*

The Deepest Levels of Forgiveness

Parents are the obstacle course in the Boot Camp of life. They are nature's way to prepare us for later battles in life.

There is a sign over the gate to a Buddhist Monastery in Tibet that once read *"Unless you've forgiven your parents, don't enter here."* That clear statement gives specific instructions to the would-be disciple of Truth: if you can't make peace with those who came before you, how can you expect to gain peace with the Divine?

"But I have forgiven my parents" you insist . . .

Have you? If so, that's great, but have you forgiven them on **all levels?** And are you even aware of the influence your ancestors exert – those beyond your parents, grandparents, great grandparents, and further back?? Are you aware that your ability to perform, your ability to achieve, and your acceptance of fulfillment are based on this influence?

It obviously helps to *consciously* forgive your parents and ancestors. There are **levels of forgiveness,** however, that lie beyond conscious awareness. They will only surface, in fact, when your inner awareness dictates.

Do you know how to read this awareness? It's not about knowing *facts* about them either. You may know *about* your ancestors but don't necessarily know their motivation, fears, or life decisions . . . that is until it is revealed by the wisdom of your own body and your own inner awareness.

Use muscle testing to get answers. You can find out, for example that there's an influence on your mother's side. You might also find an influence on your father's side. You can even test: yes, no, yes, no . . . all the way back through several generations. Find out how far it goes, what the influence is, and whether or not you can let it go or get forgiveness yourself.

Now, when you let something go – some ancestral decision or burden - it's important to *also let it go for the ancestors.* This may be important for you to accomplish personally, yes. However, there is also something larger that you are responsible for.

Embrace your past; embrace your ancestry. You can release these limitations for the ancestors, for your parents; for **all** those who came before you, as well as for your children and those who come after you.

Find peace with them and your success is assured.

CHAPTER TWENTY-SIX

The Power of Ancestry

*"The hero draws inspiration
From the virtue of his ancestors."*
- Goethe

Ancestors affect our lives and our decisions. There is, in fact, a new science of **epigenetics** which attempts to trace this phenomenon of ancestral influences on behavior.

While there may be a scientific basis for all this, this chapter is about my personal story, along with a few observations along the way.

Background

Every major religion and tradition has a lineage that ties them back to the source: God or the Creator. The power of every king depends on it. The Pope is similarly crowned and given the blessings passed down from Saint Peter. The Dalai Lama *is* the Buddha. Islam *is* the prophet Mohammed.

We secular denizens of the "New World" also have a basic need for ancestral comfort. The president of the United States, Congress, and the Supreme Court – all base their governing authority on the righteousness of the Founding Fathers, the martyrdom of Abraham Lincoln and, more recently, the sacrifices of the "Greatest Generation" – WW II veterans and families.

The Christian Bible has much to say about this ancestral power . . . and the older, the better! The *Old Testament* takes great pains in tracing the power and authority of each king and prophet to Adam and Eve, Abraham or Moses. Even the *New Testament* presents Jesus of Nazareth as the direct heir to the House of David through both parents, as descended through twenty or so generations.

The Reunion Project

Years ago, after agreeing to take on a special **family reunion** project, the subtle power of ancestors began to reveal itself to me. Although I had never had an interest in my extended family before, I selected this project as an assignment for a personal development course I was taking. I chose it, frankly, because I couldn't think of a better one. The results, however, caught me by surprise.

In the months preceding the reunion I met and became closer to several dozen cousins and relatives on my paternal grandmother's side of the family. The Wood family of South Georgia had never held such an event, however, so it took much organizing, publicizing, and hard work to put it together. We finally succeeded in hosting the first one in February of 2008, and again in 2009.

Something changed in me during the months of digging around in old newspapers and ancestral websites looking for clues to the past. I learned how my grandfather died (shot) when my father was only 10 years old, and how the secret circumstances of his death negatively affected his children and grandchildren . . . and still do to this day.

I learned how my great-great-grandfather had lost his first wife in England from childbirth; and how he came to Georgia, remarried and raised a new family. I learned of the sadness and regret he felt at having to leave his daughter behind, and how hundreds of stories – and feelings - like these are shared by generations of descendants.

I also learned that the decisions made by our ancestors – good or bad – determine not only the circumstances of our births and upbringings, but also how we think, act, and feel! Our father's, grandfather's, and great-great-grandfather's decisions STILL affect us every single day through the thoughts we have and feelings we experience. There is something akin to a thick cloud of ancestral influence floating about us as we sleep, awake, dress, eat, work and play.

I didn't know the direct power of this influence until I stood at the gravesite of my slain grandfather and experienced an unexpected wave of sadness. As a long-time agnostic, I have been reluctant to again embrace the "old time religion," so this experience was new to me.

Staring at the cold headstone, I suddenly fell to my knees. Thoughts and feelings of six generations washed over my body, mind and emotions. I wept and asked divine power for grace and the release all my ancestors and living family members from the grip of this hopeless grief.

It was towards the end of that day. As the sun set over the cemetery, I came to a peace I had not felt before - a release of something I did not understood, but intuitively held in place on behalf of ancestors I never met.

Author's Note: *Other than my own ancestors, I realized there were other "ghosts" in my early childhood – those energies that still inhabit much of Savannah and "the low country," as well as the unspoken multi-generational traumas. These same energies and traumas drove me at one point in my teens to the brink of suicide. Based on this and other experiences,*

> *I know that spirit energies dwell among us and often "speak" to those who have ears to hear.*
>
> *The things these spirits "say" can be interpreted as our own thoughts, feelings, or even just chemical reactions. Regardless, "our" thoughts have no author. Who are we anyway, if not the sum total of all energies (or chemical reactions) that are inside us and surround us? The mere knowledge of this through meditation can set us free. By the simple act of letting go of these thoughts as they arise, peace returns.*

I discovered that it's important to release not only my own ancestral influences and blocks, and to change hidden decisions that relate to them, it's also crucial to do it for the ancestors as well.

I have a friend Jim (not his real name) whose deceased mother and great grandfather on his mother's side apparently had made the decision (as determined by testing) that Jim must be responsible for, and watch over the family.

Although Jim felt strongly prompted to do this, it was against his personal preference since he fancied himself as being a kind of rebel. In wanting to do things his way, however, he discovered he was actually in alignment with his ancestors who were *also* very stubborn and liked to do things their own way as well . . .

Jim's Discovery

Jim: But I had a real surprise when we got into one part of it . . . that was really a shock to me. I mean it was just a real surprise about the influence of ancestors. Basically, we went back to the fourth generation, to my Granny's father, and there is a *huge influence* there that was clear to both of us. That he is in my physiology, on the DNA level . . . Granny's father; and I didn't know him.

Jim's wife: What was his name? . . . So you didn't know him?

Jim: No he died before I was born.

Wife: Then why was he an influence in you?

Jim: Because his influence came down to Granny and to Granny's daughter. You could see, you know how you see some things in my niece? You say "that's just like [Granny's daughter]." And me too, for mom and I knew Granny well, but my mom's grandfather - my Granny's father - I never knew him, and nobody really talked much about him.

Wife: Then how do you know him?

Jim: It was in the consciousness. And yeah, it's just, yeah it came out. For me it was a clarification of life's purpose, you know; something in me that I had been avoiding . . . that I had not believed was mine.

Michael's Commentary:

That decision that was handed down, essentially through the cellular level and possibly other ways, but that influence was enough to set Jim on a path to where he pretty much got locked in. Now for him to get free of that, we had to release his attachment to his great grandfather . . . not release his *relationship* to him, but release the *attachment to the decision* that was made, and also getting *permission* from the great grandfather to let him go.

Psychologically this has a huge impact. Whether or not physically, whether or not mystically or spiritually it has an effect, I don't know. That's not my concern, nor should it be yours.

The main concern is that the <u>results</u> you get from doing this process are important. So check to see if ancestors are influencing your decisions; influencing your ability to achieve, and influencing your relationship with other people.

CHAPTER TWENTY-SEVEN

The Role of Intuition

"There is no logical way to the discovery of these elemental laws. There is only the way of Intuition, which is helped by a feeling for the order lying behind the appearance."
- Albert Einstein

Our Link to the Cosmos

Intuition is a vital component in our lives. It helps us get what we want . . . and may also *keep* us from getting what we think we want.

Intuition is one of those unnamed things that is really hard to put a finger on. But that's what makes it intuition. That's what makes it intuitive, not "logical" in the sense we normally think of as logic. It arises and is governed by the right hemisphere of the brain – the "feeling" side.

Yet there is a hidden logic – a deeper structure to intuition that scans those **trillions of inputs** we receive inside and draws out from this well of chaotic evidence *one idea* or train of thought. When this thought springs from this well of inner knowledge, we call it **intuition.**

Intuition is not a thing. It's a state of being that is not restricted to a locale, circumstances, or even a particular person. It usually comes fully-formed and complete within itself. So, when we're speaking of intuition, we're speaking of something universal.

Intuition and the Three Selves

The gift of intuition encompasses so many things that it lies beyond our conscious capacity to accept. How, for example, do we take over *seven trillion bits of information* every minute – minute by minute, hour by hour and day by day – and distill *one thought or idea* out of all this?! *Who* in fact *guides* this process, and how does it happen so frequently??

This is where I, again, look to the ancient Hawaiians for an explanation - *via* Max Freedom Long. Long wrote that the ancients considered the *conscious mind* – they called it the middle self or *Uhane* – as the "spirit that speaks." This spirit, Long added, has a limited capacity for memory and observation, while the **Low Self** (*Ku or Unihipili*) is the one truly capable of undertaking this massive task.

As the *Ku* never forgets anything, it stands to reason that all memories are available to this being or spirit. When it therefore *"prays"* to the **High Self,** or *Aumakua,* it usually includes whatever details are necessary for evaluation by this High Self to deliver the right goods at the right time.

If the evaluation is incorrect or incomplete, the forthcoming results will reflect this error or incompleteness, causing pain, sadness, or loss. This "punishment" or "judgment" by the High Self, however, can be seen as merely the reflection of what was given it by the *Ku.*

You want results? Make sure your *Ku* is "with the program!"

How to Invoke Intuition

According to *Huna,* anything can be manifested once *Intent* is strong and persistent (conscious mind). When the *Ku* finally "gets" that you are *really committed* to something, it also acts.

The stronger your intention, the stronger is your impact on the world around you. Even if you have underlying, hidden decisions that are opposed to your desire, they will eventually give way to a constant onslaught of persistent intent.

> **Author's note:** *If the hidden decision, however, is too embedded and strong, intent may take a lifetime or may never even be realized. This is why the Logical Soul® process – and Access - is so important!*

Once the commitment is received, the *Ku* searches the memory and pulls out all files pertaining to your conscious desire. It then *prays* these files to the High Self.

Aumakua, upon hearing the prayer, "rains down benefits" in the form of a thought, idea, or insight.

In the world of manifestation, the dual forces of **intention** and **action** reign supreme. Wherein, giving the *Ku* the strong signal that you will not give up – plus the added physical proof of this intent through action - it complies with your request, generates the necessary emotion, or *mana*, and prays to the High Self.

You are Destined to Be Successful!

Use the method described above, you *will* be successful. In essence, your body and nervous system can remember everything you've ever said; and everything you've ever done and seen, everywhere you've been, and more. It can remember all the relationships you've ever had, and every thought you've ever entertained.

In the east, intuition is said to have its seat in the sixth chakra – the so-called **"third eye"** – that connects you to the Source, and is the governor of all sensory input and expression. When functioning properly, it keeps you sane and balanced.

As memories are accumulated, they are stored in your nerve cells or in brain somewhere, beyond your conscious recognition and access. And that's okay. Your conscious mind doesn't need to walk around all day long remembering everything, since by doing so you would be *completely* overwhelmed and incapacitated.

So, by design, **there is a restriction to your conscious memory and capacity.**

This restriction filters out unlimited input and helps you avoid nervous exhaustion and mental breakdown. Without these filters humans would, in fact, suffer an **evolutionary disadvantage.** If our *Ku's* suddenly poured its knowledge out to our *Uhane, we* would all become basket cases without much capacity to do anything. Unless humans also simultaneously developed the ability of laser focus, we would simply burn out and die.

In essence, intuition is that part of your memory (or that part of your body knowledge) that – through Grace from the Low & High Self - just sort of sneaks past your conscious filter and appears fully-formed in your conscious mind. You then get what I call a "hit" of intuition.

Viruses of the Mind

While the term *virus* may sound threatening, it's really not. You've lived with *mind viruses*[29] your whole life. I simply want to cover this topic now since your ability to recognize certain outside influences will greatly improve your inner strength and self-knowledge.

It can also be quite enlightening. So here's the caveat ...

Have you ever had a **"hit"** or **intuitive feeling** that you may consider as "spiritual" or even "divinely inspired"? Have you ever had a sudden strong desire to do something, go somewhere, or be with someone?

If so, that's great. Sometimes these are inspired thoughts or feelings that are very useful to you and others when acted upon.

Sometimes, however, they are not. The hits I classify as **memes**[30] or mind viruses may not even be our own memories! These ancient memes may have been picked up by someone you met, a family member you remembered or spoke to, or even a book you read or a movie you saw.

Without going into detail, I'll just say that all perceived "intuition" is not necessarily intuition of a creative kind. It could be ancient memories that are encroaching on our ability to function. It could also be a hypnotic suggestion from someone trying to influence you on a deeper level.

That being said, one of the ways I define intuition is that it is **universal** and **inclusive.** For intuition to be true intuition, it has to derive input from "The Source," or that sacred space within. Intuition is not critical. It often will not exclude our ability to make a living. Unless we're young and adventurous, it doesn't exclude our ability to be with our family, be with our loved ones, and connect with those people we love and care about.

True intuition does not *exclude* our ability to have a healthy body, healthy relationships and a healthy outlook on life. It doesn't *exclude* the world, i.e., our ability to relate to the world, to our past and future; and to the hopes, dreams, and wishes for everyone.

True intuition is **life-supporting.** It includes life, goodness, sharing, and is based on integrity. It seeks a win-win option, gives to life, and does not take it away except in times of war.[31]

So watch for memes. If you find yourself having some feelings or hits that dictate you harm others, ignore them as you would a passing irritation.

The thought *"I'm getting this intuitive hit that I must shoot this evil person"* or whatever, is *not* true intuition unless you're in combat facing a real adversary. This may simply be an ancient memory that is coming into consciousness and arising from some impulse from the past, or from the outside. If the thought strongly persists, or if your intuition is strongly developed, then look at it. Otherwise, be cautious of accepting such thoughts as real.

When in doubt, *use muscle testing* to find out the exact cause of your hits – where they are coming from. This way you can navigate; you can set the benchmarks that lead towards your goals.

You will also continue in the direction of that which you consider to be truly important in your life: your story.

CHAPTER TWENTY-EIGHT

Your Personal Story

"The story of the human race is the story of men and women selling themselves short."
- Abraham Maslow

The Kid

There was once a kid who wanted to be a superhero. He didn't know why. It was just that being a superhero was real important to him.

This boy wanted to grow up to be one of the "big guys" - get bit by a radioactive spider, struck by super cosmic rays, or survive a nuclear plant meltdown. Then he could be "super" and be up all the bullies who picked on him.

As he got older the boy realized that this thought was a little crazy, but still clung to the idea of somehow, some day, becoming "super." Eventually he gave up and sold all his comic books. He finally came to the conclusion that he was never going to be a superhero.

Later he came to accept his *superhero* as an **inner archetype** that he could embrace, to escape the self-imposed isolation of his childhood. He still *knew* he was a superhero deep down, but had to manifest it in more creative ways.

He *knew* there was an aspect of his inner life that *could not* be denied. The more he "lived into" the perception of his superhero, the more he followed his dreams. When his dreams became real he continued to use his super powers for truth, justice and the American way . . .

No Spiders Needed

All of us have a *super hero* inside somewhere. More than that, all of us have a personal story that involves essentially three archetypal characters: The **Super Hero,** the **Super Villain,** and the **Secret Identity.**

The **Super Hero** is that image of yourself that knows what you are capable of doing. It's your spiritual core, your dynamic essence that you were born with, or developed at an early age. This essence is rarely shut down, in spite of past beatings and subjugation. It remains a power inside you that demands expression.

This part knows life, knows how to blossom into life; and knows how to bring out life, and help other people to be powerful. Your superhero embodies your ability to grow, to heal, to succeed.

The opposite of that image is our **Super Villain** or inner **Judas.** This character betrays your superhero: cuts him down or makes him weaker. He brings the kryptonite and looks for ways to destroy or weaken your superhero.

Your Judas and superhero will always be ready to do battle. It's the epic story: superhero versus super villain. Good vs. Evil. Light vs. Dark. Back and forth. Forever.

Then there's the *third element* which I call the **"secret identity."** Superman had his Clark Kent. Spider-Man had his Peter Parker. Batman had his Bruce Wayne, and so forth.

The secret identity guy (or gal) is the one who shows up every day, wears the glasses, is kind of nerdy, bumbling, bumping into things, does very ordinary things, and seems a bit boring. Other people may laugh at him.

Using this character, we allow ourselves to be weak and ineffective. In fact, this "secret" identity – much as we'd like to think otherwise - is not very secret. It is, in fact, the person who most everybody sees on a daily basis. But we'd still like to think that, *deep inside* we have the superhero ready to burst forth in all his glory, defeat the Judas, and save the world.

We also know that our secret identity is *really* the mask we wear to work every day, and that *"nobody* knows who we *really* are!" This allows us to explain away our mistakes, faults, screw-ups and embarrassments. It allows us to protect our superhero – keep him or her hidden.

We bide our time until one day, *when no one suspects it,* our superhero will *spring forth in all of his or her glory* and *everyone* will know! Until that day, however, we suffer our daily indignities with a sense of stoic martyrdom.

Drop That Kryptonite!

Come on . . . *who the heck are we fooling?!*

Let's say you don't buy this whole trip about super heroes and such. That's fine. It was a great story though, huh? Being the equal-opportunity *"Meme-ster"* that I am, I allow dissent in the ranks of my readership, and even encourage it.

For those of you, however, who <u>did</u> find truth in the previous explanation, take heart. There is both rhyme and reason for my wanderings.

You see, part of the purpose in uncovering the superhero story is that it was **MY story.** *I* had those feelings. I *WAS* that boy with a secret identity. I *DID* do as much as I possibly could to (subconsciously) undermine my ability to succeed in life as the "villain." And often still do.

The difference today, however, is that I allowed my superhero to come out the closet, got rid of my secret identity, and exposed my super villain. My story – I contend – continues to have a happy ending because I'm living it consciously. As a result, I'm much happier these days than I've ever been.

I simply discovered that <u>fighting myself was a very tiring experience.</u> Plus, I could never win! I also realized that hiding behind a "secret" identity was not protecting anyone. I mean, *come on!* If my "super hero" is so super, *WHY* then would he need *protection?* He didn't. I just opened the door and cut him loose.

When I allowed myself to really see this inner charade, I could finally let out the Big Guy and feel lighter, happier, and more relaxed with other people and with myself. I also found that, without a secret ID, there was little need for a super villain either!

The whole thing was a setup – a game I invented in my need to "be somebody" from an early age. It was my story.

Variations on a Theme

So what's <u>*your*</u> story? Maybe you didn't have my same superhero-super-villain-secret-ID triumvirate. If not, what other options are there?

Actually, there are *many* **archetypes** to choose from: the father, saint, sinner, martyr, lover, mother, virgin, wizard, warrior, and so on.

Joseph Campbell, in his books and interviews [32], examined a startling variety of archetypes from which we as human beings select "our" stories.

There are even **archetypal stories** that many of us insist on living – the *Hero's Journey,* the *Story of Job,* the *Royal wedding,* and more. Hollywood thrives on such idealized fare. Most movies, in fact, are based on tried and true formulae that are sure to guarantee box office success.

While they may change the title, actors, scripts, setting, and action sequence, the same emotions and *moral* are invoked each time. The lovers meet, fall in love; get separated by forces beyond their control, miss each other terribly, then are finally reunited in the end, amidst all the splendor and sweeping violin music Hollywood can spare.

Sometimes there is a villain; sometimes not. But each loss and reunion tugs at the heart strings and brings the couples back over and over again to relive the same drama.

So what script are you running? Are you the *wounded wife* who was cheated on by her husband, and left alone to support two small children? You are zealously living the *Madonna (virgin/mother)* and *martyr* story.

Are you a young man who ran away from home and "makes it" with as many women as he can while seeking his fortune? You may be living into the *warrior/fallen angel* story, with a touch of *Casanova* until you eventually crash and burn around middle-age. Then you become what? The *suffering artist?* The *misunderstood genius?*

No matter what your story, it has been written before. The characters have changed, as has the setting, script, etc., but the emotions and moral (beliefs) stay the same.

And while this story may have been formed by real events in your past, what is the advantage of re-running these same stories over-and-over-and-over-and-over again??

One reason: we get to prove that our story is right. This "need to be right" plays right into our martyred super hero, Madonna or whichever role we assume.

Only by connecting with the hidden *lynchpin decision,* getting access to the decision-maker, and changing this decision, will we be able to break free of this vicious cycle of self-deception.

Only by making a *new decision* to <u>Be Here:</u> <u>in the body, on this planet, in the present moment,</u> can we get on with the rest of our lives.

Yes, it is YOUR story, no one else's. But your story is unique only in the sense of form and content, not context. The **context** is the **world of your archetypes.**

Think about this: We don't live through archetypes; they live through us! If the *Super Hero* is present, he has unique powers that will be unfolded only at a time and place decided by either fate or choice. If the *Wizard* lives through you, there are inner worlds to explore that only he/you can find.

Archetypal Decisions

Question: So how do you take control of your life and live consciously?

Answer: Access & change **Archetypal Decisions.**

An "archetypal decision" is a particular decision that is both hidden AND in alignment with your inner, personal (archetypal) story. While other hidden decisions may have been made later in your life, the archetypal ones are usually formulated at a very early age – at a time when your personal story was created. Consequently, most of these decisions are beyond your conscious access.

<u>The key to changing archetypal decisions</u> is to gain access to them through the *Father, Wizard, Madonna* or *Saint* of your personal story. Only the one who you trust the most has access to the innermost workings of this narrative. Only this being can allow the child access to change an archetypal decision.

Once access is gained using the *Logical Soul®* technique, then and only then can the child change things. **Only the one who made the decision can change the decision.**

So the moral of your story could be this: *"The less you need to conceal your hero, the more he shines!"*

You can write the "happily ever after" part to your story any time you choose. Why not now?

Your personal story is, in essence, *the sum total of all the decisions you've made in your life . . .* including the ones you have *yet* to make. We all have some blank pages left. And the past is gone. Start writing anew!

By the way, your new story doesn't *have* to follow the same Hollywood formula. Occasionally there are scripts that come out that break the mold and start a new formula. The hero doesn't *always* have to be beaten to a bloody pulp before he gets divine help and his strength back. Does he?

Why not get him off the streets? Maybe give him a desk job? Or one as a creative tour guide, for cryin' out loud?! He can *still* be the hero!

And you'll be happier.

CHAPTER TWENTY-NINE

The *Real* Secret of How to Achieve Anything You Want in Life

"It is not the mountain we conquer, but ourselves."
- Sir Edmund Hillary

What Do You *Really* Want?

How would you like to easily make all the money you want? Attract your ideal mate? Discover perfect health? Create a profitable business? You can do it as hundreds of others have done it . . .

Yes, I know. You've heard it all before. Hopefully, now, however, you have an understanding that it's **not** any special *technique* that will make this happen, but YOUR OWN INNER CAPACITY for attracting and accepting these things.

This limited capacity, in fact, is *the only real obstacle to having everything you want!* I want as many people as possible to experience this, so I've structured an offer at the end of this book that hopefully you will find too enticing to resist!

Meanwhile, there's plenty of red meat left on the bone. Read on…

You and Your Onion

The *Logical Soul*® is a simple and natural technique whereby *anyone* can access deep-rooted decisions, change those decisions, *eliminate self-sabotage,* and *unleash the power of your Soul to achieve your goals.* By tapping into our own archetypal stories and decisions, we can <u>transform our lives</u> and greatly *expand our inner capacity for happiness and fulfillment.*

But it won't happen overnight.

Once you change a hidden decision, there is a transformation process that takes place. Something is released, but also something else arises. That which arises is *another* decision that was hidden by the one you released before it. So you resolve one; another arises. This happens many times.

One day you notice you are peeling away layer after layer of hidden decisions, one by one, that relate to the same issue. In looking back, you see a pattern – a certain elegant logic to the process that transformed your life. I call this gradual transformation process **"peeling the onion."**

The Logical Soul®

Overcoming Self-Deception

We covered money issues in a previous chapter. In this section, I want to cover the importance of time and *peeling the onion* as an important part of your overall success strategy.

When I started to work on my money issues, I found there were layers of thoughts, fears, and concerns about money that kept arising for me. While I still tested strong for the old decisions, the new issues where slightly different. I found them to be different facets of the same problem, and noticed this was true in everyone I worked with as well.

For example, I was very good at fooling myself into thinking that I really didn't *want* money or success. I had tied certain issues together as part of the ball of chaos that I created; and found I had to unwind this ball if I were to have any chance at freedom.

I thought, as part of this self-deception, that my earning money would bring me more fame (didn't want to be bothered), spiritual loss (didn't want that either), or would show up as my father (afraid of that).

> "You can be right or you can be rich, but you can't be both."
> – **T. Harv Eker**

I also didn't like being around crowds, got overwhelmed easily, felt needy, distracted, and so on. There was always an excuse. I found that by peeling the onion, however, each layer released a different *meme,* a different hidden decision. Each of these excuses uncovered another layer of my belief fortress.

My intense desire to be alone – to basically be a hermit – was at the time also preventing me from earning money. I didn't want people to see me. I didn't want people to know what I was doing. But it's kind of difficult to hold onto this lifestyle if you want to make money or have a business. Since commerce usually thrives on the ability to communicate with other people, I was obviously creating *very good reasons* NOT to want money.

> **Author's Note:** *There are, of course, exceptions that prove hermits can also be successful. Some authors, writers and creative people are able to support themselves quite well in solitude. The ability to communicate must still be there, however. J.D. Salinger, author of* Catcher in the Rye *and other classics, passed away in 2010 at age 91, having spent most of his adult life as a recluse.*

When I finally realized I had a *very good reason* to also *want* money, a "dynamic tension" was created and the battle began. Then issues came up furiously and often. I felt overwhelmed. Fixed that. I felt crowded. Overcame that. I was afraid of facing the world as a strong person. Jumped on that. Fear of heights? Mostly gone!

Each consecutive issue seemed like (at the time they arose) an issue of life or death. But after using the technique in a targeted way, most fears simply dissolved. Even my fear of heights – something I never consciously worked on – disappeared!

And so that's how it is with peeling the onion: It seems like life or death at the time. If not, you are probably avoiding the real issue.

Short Suffering

But don't worry. Part of what the *Logical Soul®* technique provides for is what I call *short suffering*. If you can't resolve an issue in less than an hour (an in many cases, ten minutes!) then you are not doing *Logical Soul®* work.

Other techniques may drag out the pain for hours, days, months or even years. That's entirely **not** necessary. Face it quickly. Get over it quickly and completely. Done. Move on. Do you really need to feed your suffering ego in such a dramatic way?

Change Your Personal Story

Your personal story can change. By peeling away the onions of your inner programming i.e., changing hidden decisions, you finally come to the point where you begin to realize that there is a pattern. This pattern forms the basis of your inner drama – your story.

By seeing the pattern and changing multiple hidden decisions, the pattern begins to break down. Stress dissolves. You start to create new decisions and new paradigms. *A New World.*

By changing hidden decisions – especially archetypal ones – you alter the past. Then the past conflicts are no longer dragged into the present, into your day-to-day decision-making. You become free to write another script. Present tense. Knowing you can do this, where do you want to go? What do you want to create? To be?

Before, with hidden decisions telling you that you couldn't have what you wanted, you could never do enough to fill this gaping hole in your soul.

After changing hidden decisions and programs, you suddenly find that fulfillment is within your grasp – and was actually there all along! Since your new script allows for real happiness, there is no need to suffer. Suffering simply disappears.

Creation becomes the basis of your NEW personal story. You can create anything you want. You can allow, for example, the superhero within to have unlimited power to create. And this new power to create is not based on some ancient fear mixed with hope, but based on the joy of creation itself.

Why do you climb this mountain? Because you *can!*

Begin to <u>mercilessly peel back your onion of fears and resentments.</u> Find out *all* of those things that stand in the way of what you want. There is *nothing* that should stand in your way. Use the tools provided in this book.

Create who you *really* are, since who you really are essentially is what you stand for in this life . . . your strongest *INTENT.*

CHAPTER THIRTY

How to Create Powerful Goals for a Lifetime

"Just do it."
- Nike slogan

My Promise

By now, I trust that you

- **Understand** the importance of resolving hidden decisions
- **Appreciate** the tools for *Access,* and
- **Know how** to get congruent with your goals and affirmations.

Assuming you are dedicated to completing your Goals in life, you will naturally want to develop your inner skills and capacity to go further and faster than ever before. Here is your opportunity to do that.

I have created specific ways where I can walk with you hand-in-hand to peel the onion, get access, and change hidden decisions . . . and help others do the same. I will also give you the tools you need to impact your life in **five different ways:** mentally, emotionally, physically, financially, and spiritually.

If you want to be able to work with your friends and family as part of your journey into self-discovery, the Logical Soul® is the most powerful tool for transformation you can use. Use it to start unfolding success and happiness in ways you never thought possible:

- **Before,** there was no access to these deeper decisions and the power that lay behind them. You tried to do this, however, through exercises like repeating affirmations or writing down goals.
- **Now,** you can use your mind's hidden power to achieve actual, measurable results in a very short time.
- **Now** you can create an **instant iron resolve** that naturally leads you to success on all levels, and
- **Now** you can do all this in minutes – not weeks or years!

To make this possible, I have made available private Logical Soul® coaching sessions, online trainings and live workshops for those who are serious about experiencing powerful breakthroughs!

If you like working with others, you might want to become a coach yourself! Check out our free training and paid coach training courses at www.LogicalSoul.com for a taste of how it works.

Also visit www.MyCoachTraining.com for really great articles, downloads, products, interviews with experts (in our *Mighty Mentor Series*), local Meetup groups, and workshops scheduled from time to time. I am constantly creating training materials and courses for Life and Business coaches and consultants to use in change lives for the better.

If you would like a rewarding new career, consider taking the step to become certified as a Life Coach. **Dr. Ron Owens** can start you out on his dynamic tried-and-true approach for changing lives, also through www.mycoachtraining.com.

As a health professional or certified Life Coach using advanced methods like the *Logical Soul®,* you will transform the way people think and feel. You will also start experiencing more happiness, better health and increased wealth yourself... not a bad trade-off!

Here's the deal: I want everyone to experience the *feeling of freedom and happiness* inside that comes with knowing you can - at any moment – be free of suffering and self-sabotage. Since you are one of the select few in the world who now understand this work, you are invited to join my Transformation Team. Simply learn how to share this work with others!

I have poured over twenty years and tens of thousands of dollars into developing training materials around this unique method of self-discovery, so naturally I want to share it with the whole world. But for this I need your help!

It really starts with you. So plant and water that **Seed of Success** today, and I hope to meet you in person soon to hear about your amazing breakthroughs!

To Your Success,
- Michael Craig

APPENDIX A

How To Use Logical Soul® Method

NOTICE & DISCLAIMER: *This material is the property of Michael Craig and Logical Soul LLC and is provided for the sole purpose of self-help, and to educate coaches, doctors and professions who work with others. The material in this book is not to be used as therapy, or to treat anyone for any disease or dysfunction unless you are fully licensed to do so.*

The Logical Soul® is a simple, natural technique for uncovering hidden decisions that block your health, wealth and happiness, changing these decisions, and allowing you to move forward in life without struggle.

The process itself is made up of Four Steps:
1. Interview
2. Discovery
3. Access
4. Resolution

Each of these phases is unique in and of itself and, while the phases are usually presented in order, they sometimes present themselves in unique and random ways. Testing and feedback is important throughout the process to discovery which phase you are in, and what is needed at each point.

The Interview and Discovery phases, for example, may become interchangeable. You may think you know the key issue, only to discover in the testing phase that more information (Interview) is needed. The same is true as you go through the process.

You may find that the interview reveals that a Forgiveness or Amends Process is necessary before you can even get results from muscle testing.

The Logical Soul® process takes years to perfect. Although you can have a working knowledge of how to use it, it will take time to get a "feel" for both the process and each of the clients or people who come to you. Be patient; this technique – once mastered – will open doors to transformation that can change lives forever!

INTERVIEW

The Logical Soul® Interview is the first in a series of steps. The purpose of this phase is to allow the person's conscious and subconscious minds to relax, trust you, and open up. Although there are no clear steps to follow, by listening a certain way and using a series of questions – each one digging a little deeper than the one before it, about 5 questions deep – allows the subconscious mind to feel some respect that allows it to tell you things it wouldn't ordinarily share.

DIVINE LISTENING. This is the process of letting your ego go and trusting that the person sitting in front of you is a Divine Being who is playing a game of cat-and-mouse with him or herself. Their conscious mind wants something. The subconscious mind, on the other hand, wants something completely different . . . and for a VERY GOOD REASON! You job as a Divine Listener is to respect the Divine Being in front of you and listen for that hidden good reason.

DISCOVERY

The Logical Soul® Discovery is a "motivational cybernetics" tool you can use to communicate with your "subconscious being" or "Ku." Only by this process can you begin to see the discrepancies between conscious and subconscious decisions, and allow new subconscious decision to be made that align with your stated goal.

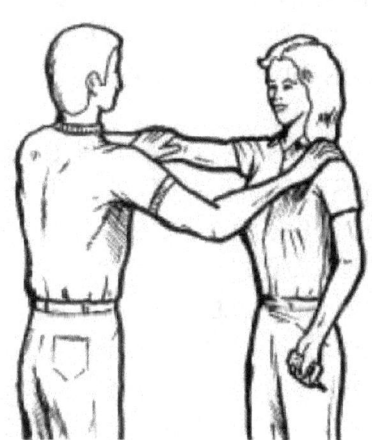

Once you discover a conscious-subconscious conflict, the Discovery process allows both you and your clients to get instant feedback. Test each one while digging deeper in an attempt to find THE "Lynchpin Decision" that holds the so-called "problem" in place.

Muscle Testing is done by asking the person to stretch out his or her arm to the side, usually palms down. I usually test standing behind and slightly to the side of the person (some people like to test from the front; either way is OK). I put one hand on their shoulder, just to stabilize the Deltoid muscle, and the other hand on the wrist. Using 3 fingers on the wrist, I ask the person to make the statement I want to test. Once the statement is made, I say "Hold," wait 2-3 seconds, then press downwards with about 3 pounds of pressure. The muscle will either respond as strong (yes) or weaker (no). **If Not:** *check for Forgiveness, Amends, or being "out of the body."*

Using this 3-3-3 testing process, ask the person to say several things you both know are true while testing. Each of these should register strong, or "yes." Do this until you both feel comfortable, then test some false statements until you both can see the difference between weak and strong. Then you're ready to go.

The reason why conscious-subconscious conflicts exists is because the communication between your conscious being ("the spirit who speaks," or *Uhane*) and subconscious being (*Ku*) has broken down.

While in the Discovery Phase, use STATEMENTS that are both SPECIFIC and PRESENT-TENSE. This allows the *Ku* to either APPROVE them (based on the desire to please), or DISAPPROVE (based on the power of a pre-existing Prime Directive). Vague statements that involve "want," need," "wish" or "should" are confusing to the subconscious since they are not decisions, but indicate lack and are therefore to be avoided.

Use instead statements like:
> I CHOOSE to be here – in the body, on the planet (or whatever the lynchpin statement is)
> I CHOOSE Happiness,
> I AM Worth ($ money),
> I CAN Accept ($ money), or
> I EASILY EARN ($ money) in the presence of my Father . . . etc.

Here is how you help formulate these statements.

Ask your client:

The Logical Soul®

"As I understand it, you have an issue with _____. Assuming it is possible to override this decision or programming, here is my question:
'What is a statement you can make that, if true in the present tense, would mean that the problem or issue no longer exists as a problem?' or

'What Statement could you make that would render this issue – and all the difficulties that come with it - harmless?'"

By testing statements and getting a Yes or No answer, you are able to clarify the issue on a much deeper level by testing further underlying issues or statements. Once you get THE STATEMENT that encompasses ALL parts of the issue, you will have found the LYNCHPIN DECISION. This is the goal of Discovery.

ACCESS

The Access Phase is unique to the Logical Soul®. Instead of trying to out-maneuver and go around "sticky problems," or issues that block one's ability to achieve, Access bestows upon the Subconscious Being (*Ku* or Low Self) the honor of allowing (or not allowing) access to the very survival decision that has held the so-called problem in place until now.

The reason why Access may *NOT* be available in the first place is because the *Ku* has taken responsibility to fulfill a direct order from the Conscious Being (*Uhane*) that
     a) This is a survival situation, and
     b) Once this decision is made, do NOT allow it to be changed!

Consequently, this "Prime Directive" from an immature child (or through parental or ancestral influence) is tucked away deep within the subconscious, and away from conscious awareness or control. The only way to gain Access is through TRUST of the one who made the original decision, and PERMISSION from original decision-maker(s) to make a NEW decision to counter-act the original one.

Once you've established the Lynchpin Decision, muscle test the subject or client while having them say:
1. "Access is available to change this program," and
2. "I allow (client's name) access to change this program."

If both statements are true, proceed to the Resolution Phase.

If #1 is true, but #2 is false, that means that the client's conscious mind (Uhane) is locked out. You must gain the trust of the client's Ku in order to determine his or her personal Archetype, Protector or Guide. Once done, proceed to Resolution. (By the way, #2 cannot be true unless statement #1 is true also.)

If both statements are false, you will need to find out WHO has Access (personal Archetype, Protector or Guide) and get this being or Guide to "open the door" to the underlying decision(s). You can also use the Alternative Access Process, i.e., the "Family Conference" to get Access, or in some cases, the Forgiveness Process.

The Logical Soul®

RESOLUTION

The purpose of this phase is to allow the Inner Child - or "The One Who Made the Decision" – an opportunity to change that decision on a very deep level... AND bring it into the body so as to make it more concrete and manifest in everyday life. Below is a script used in most cases:

Ask the child if he or she is ready to make a NEW decision about   [the issue]...   If so, describe the following:

"Take your child by the hand and go up to a place somewhere there is a very colorful Rainbow Path leading off into the distance. Take your child by the hand (and have his or her other guide – parent or guardian – take the other hand) and begin to walk down this path. At the end of that path, you and the child begin to notice there is a very large, elaborate Gate at the end. It begins to open... slowly ... and you notice there is a very bright light on the other side of the gate.

"As the gate opens more and more, you notice the light gets brighter and brighter until, finally, it is completely open and the light shines on both (or all) of you... and you are covered with this brightness from top to bottom, head to toe.

"Squeeze your child's hand as you walk towards this light, and explain to the child that this is a Place of Decision, and that he or she will have an opportunity to make a New Decision on the other side. Explain that – as soon as he or she gets to the threshold and steps over into the other side, HE (SHE) WILL HAVE

MADE A NEW DECISION THAT [Affirmation or New Decision].

"So finally you reach the threshold. Say to the child 'Whenever you are ready, step over the threshold and I will follow.' Then tell me when the child does this….. he (she) does? Good. Now cross that threshold with him (her), get down and look him (her) in the eyes and say to him (her)…'THANK YOU for making this new decision! Thank you for having the courage to do this! I need you and couldn't do it without you! '

"Then open up your heart and ask the child to come inside – tell the child you will protect him (her) from now on, and that they will have your support and help at all times. Tell the child that he or she only needs to ask and you will provide – as best you can – what they need. Then seal up your heart and feel them inside – happy and fulfilled – then go to the edge of this place and look down to see the earth as a small globe below, with a silver chord running down from this place.

"At some point, make a decision to jump onto this chord and glide down towards the Earth... it gets bigger and bigger the closer you get until, finally, you zip on by the clouds, through the top of the roof... through the top of your head... into your head, your neck, your shoulders, your chest, your abdomen... hips, thighs, knees, legs, ankles and feet. Then feel the Earth beneath your feet, as the energy shoots down and connects to the center of the Earth, shoots back up... up through your feet, legs, thighs…. and into your Solar Plexus, where the energy creates a vortex of purple light that begins to circulate throughout your body . . . all the tissues, cells, and organs of the body . . . with a NEW DECISION ... {Affirmation or Decision}...

"With this new decision firmly established throughout your body... all the tissues, cells and organs... take a deep breath, and open your eyes."

[RE-TEST]

ACCESS/RES. ALTERNATIVE: THE FAMILY CONFERENCE

"Since your Ancestors are involved in creating or holding in place the underlying decision, let's hold what we call a 'Family conference.' This allows your tribal connections to be cleared, and new decisions to be made without fear.

"Picture yourself at the head a large room – a conference room – where you are standing on the podium or seated at the front with either a microphone, or a way that everyone in the room can hear you. Slowly, your ancestors (from either your father or moth's side, or both) begin to come into the room and find a place to sit down. You've never seen these people, except through old photographs, but you know them . . . they are your ancestors, the ones whose genes surge through your body in this life.

"Allow them all to come in and be seated. At some point, call the room to attention and present your greeting: 'I want to thank all of you for coming here at my request. I also want you to know that I *really appreciate* your doing this, and that I owe you my life – *literally*. I realize most or all of you have gone through tremendous pain, suffering and challenges in your life, and that there is no way I can thank you enough for these sacrifices. But please allow me to express appreciation in my own small way, and to say I treasure being your descendant. I hope to honor you by living a great life – one that carries forth the same dreams and wishes to my heirs that you have bestowed upon me.

"'I want to say, however, that I'm having a problem right now that I need your help with. I have come across an inner decision that is blocking me from moving forward: _____(repeat the decision)_____. And, because of my need to be connected to you – as my tribe, my ancestors, and to honor your place in my life - I have subconsciously chosen to hold on to this decision as if it were my own.

"'But now I need your *PERMISSION* and *BLESSING* to let go of this decision, and make a NEW DECISION for the sake of my life and the lives of my children and/or heirs. Again, please let me know what you need in order to grant me your *PERMISSION* and your *BLESSING* that I might change this decision. I'm not asking for YOU to release this believe or decision; I only ask that *I may be allowed to make my own new decisions* about how life is, and the way I should live it.'

"At this point, notice how your ancestors in the room begin to respond. Are they agreeable? Not? Allow them to either raise an objection or approve. If they approve, say 'Thank you for your permission and blessings that I might let go of this tremendous burden.' (The full process is taught in LS Training)

APPENDIX B

The Logical Soul® Forgiveness Process

(Edited from a transcript of a radio show presentation, *Logical Soul Talk* with Michael Craig, May 19, 2009)

...If there's something in your past that you have that is unresolved, or if you haven't forgiven somebody or you had some traumatic experience that you've dealt with in the past that's not been resolved consciously, the subconscious being doesn't know how to deal with it except to just store it and to do what the Huna calls *ruminate* about that particular issue. The low self doesn't have the same conscious logical approach to dealing with issues.

The importance of the Logical Soul® is to basically bring to the surface these particular issues that are unresolved . . . not just to look at them, experience something, cry, or beat a pillow or something like that, but to actually look at the decisions that took place at the moment in which these incidences got stuck into place.

Whatever comes up, just feel that issue, feel that – what we call "stuff" (my wife calls it stuff). Just feel the stuff, feel the issue, feel the emotion, e.g. anger.

Forgiveness does not mean letting whoever abused you off the hook. What it does is balance the energy and allow your inner child (or adult) to feel that "justice is served." So if there were something going on that you did not forgive at some point in your life, it's very important to balance the energy there.

Often that means going back and **giving back to that person exactly what they gave to you.** If they hit you, go back and hit them. If they did you wrong, go back and do them wrong, and so forth.

Now, a lot of times you don't feel this is appropriate because you were taught as a kid that no, this is not appropriate. You were taught you shouldn't do this and blah, blah, blah. However, understand this is not the logic of the soul. The logic of the soul is, "if you do something to me, I'm going to do it to you." Period!

Without doing that, the child, or whoever made that decision, will not feel resolved – often for a long period of time - and you'll feel stuck in that resentment. So, the process of forgiveness means going back and "balancing the scales" so that the child can break through that resentment and allow its own form of logic to prevail. This way you can resolve any form of anger and resentment quickly.

I discovered this technique actually in the 5th grade, I was in the 5th grade in Savannah, Georgia– I guess it was in 1962, something like that. I was about 10 years old.

And of course, my grandmother was a born-again Christian and she always taught to turn the other cheek, forgive your enemies and always do this and this. And because I loved my grandmother and always wanted to do what she said, I never wanted to be anything other than a good boy and a real

Christian, and be the best I could be. Which, of course, I was. That is until I started getting picked on at school.

I'll never forget, this one guy used to pick on me all the time. His name was Bobby...I'll never forget him. And he use to pick on me mercilessly and it just bugged the heck out of me. I just didn't know what to do with him and I didn't know what to do with the situation because I couldn't hit him, I couldn't fight back because obviously, I wasn't being a good Christian if I did.

So, I was becoming more and more frustrated and more and more – I didn't know what. I couldn't figure it out and Mimi really didn't have an answer for me either.

I remember lying in bed one night and asking God, "what do I do, what do I do?" Suddenly this feeling came over me, like I just wanted to kill Bobby . . . I just want to tear him to shreds!

Then I just remember closing my eyes and just stabbing him, and shooting him, and crucifying him... I just did all these horrible things to him.

And I soon fell asleep. The next day I remember I went to school and I felt a whole lot better. I remember paying attention to this feeling and an amazing thing happened . . . Bobby didn't pick on me that day. Nor the day after that! In fact, I don't think Bobby ever picked on me again!

As a matter of fact, he became quite civil as I recall, or he just got bored and just ignored me, I don't remember . . . but neither do I remember having a fight or being picked on by Bobby after that particular incident.

The whole thing was that, by having anger present in my subconscious, I sort of had an antenna sticking up over my head going, *"Here I am Bobby; please come kick me and push my books, and do all the horrible things to me that you can because I have all this non-forgiveness going on."*

Here I was thinking all the time I forgave him when in fact I had not. Consciously I was forgiving him. Subconsciously, there were a lot of unresolved issues going on with this bully that I just couldn't let out because I trying to be such a good "Christian."

By the way, I'm not recommending anyone go out and shoot or hurt people! All I'm saying is that there is a type of negative energy present in your nervous system and in your mind, and that if it remains unresolved, it will torment you. But there are some people who think that doing this process is bad . . . like it will put out bad vibes, or send a curse to somebody, or that it's like some form of witch craft or something.

To answer that, I would say that your thoughts are *already* there, your resentments are already present. You *already* have this anger and this unresolved resentment towards this person. If it is not brought to the surface and let out, it will become a poison . . . and not only poison you but also poison the other person as well.

There are a few other aspects to this technique but that's the essence of it. It can be done anytime you really feel resentment towards someone.

APPENDIX C

The Logical Soul® Amends Process

Amends is the opposite of Forgiveness in many ways, but they share something in common: *lack of forgiveness*. While Forgiveness is outer-directed, i.e., aimed at correcting the perceived injustice from outside insults or being hurt by others, the AMENDS Process is inner-directed. This process seeks to correct the perceived injustice of you hurting another.

Huna, in fact, says the only sin is to hurt another. The reason is because hurting others brings shame on the Ku, and forces it to hide (if consciousness is high enough), or become insensitive to others (if consciousness drops or becomes de-sensitized, as in war or genocide).

To do an Amends Process it is first important in Discovery to show that shame is, indeed, present, and that Amends is required before clearing can happen.

Many times the lack of forgiveness is for something <u>perceived by someone else as being hurtful – when in fact it was not</u>. This happens a lot when a child is scolded for "not respecting your father," or "asking too many questions," or doing other things that are natural to the child, but were perceived by the adult as a "sin." In such cases, it is important to feel the "injustice" in the body, and test to see if this feeling actually belongs to you . . . or if you simply took it on from your parents or elders.

Often that's all it takes. If not, go back to the very first time you felt this way. By getting in touch with the feelings and decisions, you can use the regular 4-step process to resolve this.

If, on the other hand, you really *DID* do harm to someone else (killed, robbed, embezzled, kidnapped, sexually, verbally, or otherwise abused another), it is important to know that your *Ku* or subconscious being will carry this shame until you make amends for your actions. This process is so important it is one of the major steps in Alcoholics Anonymous (AA) and many other 12-Step programs.

By admitting you wronged or harmed another, then taking steps to <u>truly</u> correct this imbalance, you take a huge step towards inner peace, and feeling the goodwill of others. Without taking these steps, you will remain in a state of shame and guilt.

So HOW to you make a mends to someone who it may be impossible to make amends to? This was the question posed to Mahatma Gandhi by a Hindu who killed a Muslim child during a riot in India and said he "lives in Hell." Gandhi replied simply "I know a way out of Hell: Take a Muslim child who has lost his parents – an orphan – and raise him as your own."

Gandhi then added, *"But be sure to raise him as a Muslim."*

The outer actions you take must reflect your desire to cleanse the shame you feel inside. Whatever actions accomplish this end (and you can muscle test to find out), then do those things.

FOOTNOTES

CHAPTER ONE

[1] Taken from www.QuotesDaddy.com. It has no annotation as to its origin, but a similar version appears in Fuller's *Critical Path* (1981 Ed., p. 277) as "Pollution is simply energy – in the form of unfamiliar matter – which the timing of the omniregenerative cosmic system cannot immediately use but must use later."

[2] Ehrenreich, Barbara, *Bright-Sided: How the Relentless Promotion of Positive Thinking Has Undermined America*, 2009, p. 5.

[3] Fuller quote from *CJ Fearnley's Favorite Quotes and Poems*, at www.cjfernley.com.

CHAPTER THREE

[4] *Mozart as Teacher*, by Alfred Mann and Mario Mercado, quoted from an article posted at www.musicassociatesofamerica.com.

CHAPTER FOUR

[5] Maslow, A.H., A *Theory of Human Motivation* (*Psychological Review*, 50, 370-396; 1943)

[6] Some newer Maslow charts show *eight levels*: 1-Biological and Physiological needs, 2-Safety needs, 3-Belongingness and Love needs, 4-Esteem Needs, 5-Cognitive needs, 6-Aesthetic needs, 7-Self-actualization, and 8-Transcendence.

[7] Research on the *Transcendental Meditation*^{TM} (TM) technique between 1970 and 1975 laid the foundation for subsequent brain research that challenged the limited waking-sleeping-dreaming model of consciousness. I only chose to talk about TM here because I am most familiar with it, not because it is the only way to induce coherence. You can find other, more recent non-TM heart-brain research at www.heartcoherence.com, along with explanations of various techniques that induce coherence.

[8] Transcendental Meditation, self-actualization, and psychological health: A conceptual overview and statistical meta-analysis, *Journal of Social Behavior and Personality* 6: 189248, 1991.

[9] For more information on TM and Maharishi, visit *www.tm.org*.
[10] From the Author's notes while with Maharishi in Villars, Switzerland in 1973.
[11] Taylor, Jill Bolte, PhD., *My Stroke of Insight: a Brain Scientist's Personal Journey* (Viking Penguin, 2006)
[12] Ibid., p. 82.

CHAPTER FIVE
[13] "Energy Limits to the Computational Power of the Human Brain" by Ralph C. Merkle, *www.foresight.org*, No. 6, Aug. 1989. Also see "How Many Bytes in Human Memory?" No. 4, October 1988.

CHAPTER SEVEN
[14] Ibid.

CHAPTER NINE
[15] Horace Walpole coined "serendipity" after getting the inspiration from a Persian fairy tale, "The Three Princes of Serendip," whose heroes often made discoveries by chance.

CHAPTER ELEVEN
[16] King, Serge Kahili, Huna *and Hawaiians*. Online article excerpt & edited.
[17] Max Freedom Long, *The Secret Science At Work* (DeVorss & Co. Publishers, 1953 ed.), p. 84.
[18] Ibid., page 85

CHAPTER THIRTEEN
[19] *Virus of the Mind* (Integral Press, 1996) by Richard Brodie. This book is a powerful introduction to the concept of *Memes*.

CHAPTER SEVENTEEN
[20] Ori Bengal is a web guy, photographer, and adventurer, but bills himself primarily as the "Couch Surfer" because he stays with people at their homes and helps them with marketing, promotion, web design and other services. www.couchsurfingori.com.
[21] Notes by Author from a lecture by Marshall Thurber in 1988.

CHAPTER TWENTY-THREE
[22] Margaret Mahler's 1975 groundbreaking observations, as reported in *Love Me, Touch Me, heal Me* by Erica Goodstone, PhD (www.createhealingandlovenow.com).

CHAPTER TWENTY-FOUR
[23] Originally published in Germany in 1946 as *Ein Psycholog erlebt das Konzentrationslager;* published as *Man's Search for Meaning* by Beacon Press in 1959.
[24] Wikipedia.
[25] *Expelled: No Intelligence Allowed*, by Ben Stein (2008); a video documentary about the clash between the memes of Darwinian evolution and those of intelligent design.
[26] See **Chapter 8**

CHAPTER TWENTY-FIVE
[27] See *Mental Floss* magazine, March-April, 2009, Volume 8, issue 2, pp. 54-57. www.mentalfloss.com. Apparently, genetic tendencies can be handed down to us based on experiences and decisions our parents and ancestors had or made during their lifetimes. This sudden deviation from **Darwin** came about after the **Human Genome Project** showed that our sheer complexity existed despite having far fewer genes than we originally expected. This discovery resurrects some of the theories set down in biology in the early 1800's by **Jean-Baptiste Lamark.** See www.epigenome.org for more information.
[28] Ibid.

CHAPTER TWENTY-SEVEN
[29] *Virus of the Mind* by Richard Brodie.
[30] Ibid.
[31] In such a wartime situation, intuition is based on the sworn duty – or prime directive - of a soldier or fighter to defend his family, his country, or his people. This is a case where intuition and reflexive action combine to create action that is appropriate for battle conditions. If you have to think about it, there is only one decision - pull the trigger or die. Pausing at this moment to ponder the paradox, you choose – by default – to die.

CHAPTER TWENTY-EIGHT

[32] *The Power of Myth* and other books by Dr. Joseph Campbell. Dr. Campbell was also part of a TV interview series with Bill Moyers in the early 1990's.

INDEX

A

AA (Alcoholics Anonymous)   199
Aaron, Raymond   V, 166
ability   IX, 7, 15, 19, 22, 29, 47, 51-2, 80, 93, 99-101, 105, 117,
    120, 122, 132, 158, 168, 176, 180, 186, 197, 218, 227, 233-4,
    239, 241, 250, 261
act(s)   30, 36, 92, 145, 162, 184, 188-9, 204, 207, 223, 225, 231
action   XIV, 3, 8-9, 16, 18-20, 22-3, 25-6, 29, 38, 46, 55-6, 62, 85-6,
    91, 105, 162, 168-9, 171, 173, 177, 182, 188, 195, 199, 200,
    203-4, 207-8, 232, 242, 272, 275
acupuncture   III, 60, 79-80
addiction   74, 92, 183, 188, 194, 199
adult mind   113-4, 178
affirmation(s)   3, 7-8, 15, 20, 31, 44, 46-7, 53-4, 86, 88-9, 109-111,
    113, 118, 120-1, 123, 129, 136-7, 139, 141, 143, 146, 148, 150,
    155-8, 162-3, 169, 253-4
age(s)   7, 16, 64, 70-1, 128, 196, 198, 209-10, 250
  early   119, 196, 238, 241, 244
  enlightened   182
  middle   243
  new   40, 60-1, 83
  of Enlightenment   75
  young   194-5, 197
AK (applied kinesiology)   52, 60, 89, 111, 142, 144, 180
alignment   X, 20, 22, 54, 149, 169, 180-9, 275, 244
ancestors   VII, X, 3-4, 49, 152, 195, 208, 213, 215, 218-9, 221-5,
    227, 265-6, 275
ancestry   219, 221
anger   38, 61, 83, 126, 143, 182-3, 267-270
anxiety   V, 46, 62, 263
applied kinesiology - *see* AK
archetypal   205, 238, 242, 244, 248, 251
Archetypal Decisions   - See Decisions
archetypes   151, 181, 242-3
Arjuna   199
arm   53, 89, 99, 110, 142
asymmetry   36
attraction   8, 156
  body's   60
  law of   V, 158, 162
Aumakua   99, 101, 106, 157, 230-1
Awareness   IX, 37, 71, 200, 218, 262
  inner   103, 218

B

barriers   40, 62, 118-9, 182
baseball players   205
Beagle   149-150
beast   190
Beate   VII, 39
Belief(s)   11-12, 29, 32, 52, 149, 170, 180, 207-9, 211, 213, 243, 250
benchmarks   29, 38, 163, 167-8, 170-1, 173, 235
birth   122, 175, 216, 223
birth mother   194
birth parents   195
blessings   78, 216-7, 221
body   IX, 3, 9-10, 18, 41, 45, 48-9, 51-5, 60-5, 68, 71-4, 80, 87-8, 90, 100, 104, 116, 125-6, 128, 133-4, 136, 139, 146, 155-6, 158, 164-5, 169-171, 173, 188-9, 211, 218, 224, 232-4, 239, 243, 259-260, 263-5, 267, 269-271
body knowledge   233
body memory   - See Memory, body
boss   135-6
boy   17, 80-1, 237-8, 241
boyfriend   55, 62, 181
brain(s)   IX, X, 36-8, 45, 63, 78, 140, 232, 273-4
  left   38, 49
  right   38, 48-9, 52, 54, 229
brainwaves   2
break   7, 26, 30, 91, 184, 209, 243, 245, 251
breathe   11, 28, 6, 128
Brigitte   II, 1, 82, 109-116
brushing   204, 206
burning   79, 81, 94, 98, 216
burning desire   25-6, 28, 30-31
business   2, 17, 27, 37, 51, 59-60, 78, 127, 129, 148, 171-3, 179-180, 182, 205, 247, 250, 255

C

capacity   VIII, 2, 54, 64, 75, 93, 145, 230, 233, 248, 253
  inner   247-8
Cathy   59-62, 66, 82, 151, 179-182
cells   156, 193, 232
century   64, 82, 186, 259
change   V, VII, IX, X, XI, 1-3, 5-6, 8-9, 27, 29, 39, 43, 45-8, 54, 56-7, 61, 64-5, 73, 80, 86-7, 98, 105-7, 113-6, 120, 123, 129-130, 133, 136-7, 144, 148, 150-3, 155-9, 165, 168, 172, 180, 183, 193, 195-7, 201, 206, 215, 223, 225, 242-4, 248, 251, 256-8, 261-3, 266
Changeable Defaults   201
characters   67-70, 190, 238-9, 243
chemical reactions   224

child   9-10, 16, 39, 46, 76, 105-6, 115-6, 127-8, 151-3, 155, 164-5, 177-8, 181, 196-7, 210, 244
   inner   100, 106, 177
childbirth   223
childhood   III, 100, 134, 177, 181, 185, 188, 196, 224, 238
children   10, 114, 178, 197, 210, 219, 223, 242, 266
chiropractic   III, 61, 77-8, 81, 165, 182, 196
chiropractor   VIII, 52, 60, 80, 142-3, 180
clients   III, 1, 36-7, 125, 135, 158, 163, 183, 194, 196, 255
coach   VIII, 121, 172-3
coaching   254
coherence   36, 265
command   46, 100, 104, 177
computer   148
Computerized Voice Stress Analysis – See CVSA
Condition(s)   37, 39, 47, 54, 74, 81, 111, 165, 275
conditioned   178
conflict   3, 9, 35, 37, 85-6, 105, 188, 251
conflicting   209, 211
congruent   2, 19-21, 23, 27-8, 39, 51, 97-8, 163, 173, 253
connect   X, 128, 156-7, 191, 194, 211, 232, 234, 243
connections   2, 22, 98, 215-7
conscious decisions   9, 22, 40, 45, 177
conscious mind   9, 49, 63, 65, 89-90, 99-100, 104-6, 113, 115, 150, 157, 169, 182, 188-9, 230-3
consciousness   36, 45, 56, 60, 86, 102-4, 135, 161, 186, 198, 201-2, 211-213, 226, 235, 271, 273
context   207, 243
control   35, 46, 63, 78, 94, 98, 105, 159, 186-8, 196, 198, 208-9, 242, 244, 262
cost   10, 11, 114, 125, 144
create   XI, 1, 3-4, 10, 21, 30, 40, 43, 57, 69, 71, 83, 90, 102, 129, 156-7, 179, 183-4, 189, 199, 205, 217, 244, 247, 249-254, 264, 275
creation   28, 207, 252
critical decisions   66
culture   12, 95, 102, 203, 214-5
CVSA (Computerized Voice Stress Analysis)   142, 144

D

dad   - See father
death   43, 78, 129, 178, 203, 205-6, 216, 223, 250-1
debt   83, 103
deception, self-   12, 243, 249
decision-maker   93, 243
decision(s)   VII, IX, X, 2-3, 8-10, 14, 21, 22-3, 26-7, 30-1, 35-6, 39-41, 44-7, 49, 52-4, 57, 61, 64-6, 69-70, 73, 76, 78-9, 82, 87, 100-1, 15-7, 115-6, 122, 124, 126, 128-130, 133, 136, 139, 141,

143, 148-153, 155-9, 164-5, 167-171, 173, 177-9, 181-3, 188-9, 193-200, 211, 213-215, 218, 223, 225-7, 231, 243-5, 248-9, 251-4, 257, 259-268, 272, 275
  ancestral   39, 213, 215, 218
  ancient   106
  archetypal   151, 244
  deep-rooted   248
  emotion-based   164
  emotion-survival-based   45
  great-great-grandfather's   223
  hidden   VII, IX, 2-3, 14, 21, 26-7, 30-1, 35, 41, 45-7, 61, 64-5, 67, 87, 100, 106, 124, 129, 133, 136, 141, 143, 153, 155, 158-9, 168, 171, 178-9, 193-5, 211, 214-215, 225, 231, 244, 248-9, 251-4
  key   64, 151
  limiting   152
  lynchpin   150-1, 243
  major   76, 122
  new   107, 116, 152, 155-8, 164, 182, 243, 251
  original   106
  particular   155, 244
  right   173
  subconscious   9
deity   200, 202
determinism   186, 189
detox   3
  mind/mental   9-10, 12, 14-15, 51
development   VII, 36, 173, 177, 195-6, 222
dialogue, inner   3, 85-6, 88
direction   VI, 6, 42, 105-6, 179, 235, 254
directive, prime   10, 105-7, 121, 152, 157-8, 178, 182, 197, 260, 262, 275
disappointment   121, 125-6, 143
disciple   199, 217
discover   VII, 2-3, 8, 14, 27-8, 31, 38, 45, 54, 56, 59, 62, 70, 78, 88, 93-5, 98-100, 118, 124-5, 129-130, 137, 142, 145, 150-2, 155, 164, 181-2, 194, 225, 241, 247, 257, 259
discovery   VII, 45, 59, 62, 77, 82, 109, 129, 131, 136, 137, 139, 145, 150, 179, 225, 229, 255, 257, 259-261, 271, 275
doctors   II, 53, 60, 80, 143, 175-7, 182, 184, 190, 199
  medical   II, 143, 177
dollars, million   7, 91-3, 169
dreams   141, 189, 234, 238
Drenda   77-8
Drive(n)   7, 28, 55, 187, 190, 206, 213
drugs   11, 73, 176

E

early age   119, 196, 238, 241, 244
earn   7, 83, 112, 168, 170, 198
earning   93, 145-6, 170, 249-250
earth   71-2, 82, 101-2, 156
ego   101-2, 132, 134, 188, 209
elders   68, 70, 209, 215
elephant   209
emotions   IX, 41, 49, 52, 87-8, 100, 165, 178, 183, 224, 242-3
employees   172
energies   156, 182, 224
enlightenment   75, 199
entity   101, 104, 149
epigenetics   221
error(s)   21, 54, 68, 159, 231
essence   18, 52, 105-6, 151, 178, 232-3, 238, 245
events   VII, 46, 56, 75, 80, 129, 204, 207, 211, 243
experiment/experimental   54, 62, 104, 143-4

F

failure   III, 4, 8-9, 11, 13, 26, 28, 37, 41, 44, 51-2, 86, 97, 117-122, 125-6, 128-9, 139, 143, 151, 161, 170, 191, 205, 256
family   II, X, 22, 35, 46, 49, 73, 89, 110, 122, 125, 132, 176, 188, 200, 207-8, 210, 213-215, 217, 222-5, 234, 267
father   III, VI, 101, 177, 188, 199, 214, 218, 223, 225-6, 234, 254, 262, 265, 275
  founding   221
  grand   223, 226
  great grand   225-6
  great-great grand   214, 223
fear   V, VII, 10-11, 20, 35, 46, 72, 105, 125-6, 133-4, 158, 162, 172-3, 178, 181-4, 190, 205, 211, 218, 249-250, 252, 265, 273
feedback   53-4, 56, 60, 63, 88-9, 132, 143, 172, 181, 197
  bio   52, 88
  inner   172
  instant   125, 139-141
field   28, 31, 36-7, 60, 173, 175, 182, 186
fight   5, 20, 21, 94, 110, 148, 162, 241, 269-270
finger(s)   53, 81, 90-1, 110, 179, 229
  index   90-1
food   35, 55, 6, 206
forgiveness   217-218
free will   185-7, 189, 214-5
freedom   4, 78, 140, 186, 211, 249, 255
  Max ___ Long - See Long, Max Freedom
Freud   94, 102-3, 186, 207
fulfillment   19-20, 55, 147, 158, 173, 197, 218, 248, 252
Fuller, R. Buckminster   5, 11, 15

G

gate   156, 217
generation(s)   VII, X, 214, 218, 221-5
George   69, 85, 111, 142
Georgia   II, III, V, VII, VIII, 1, 77, 83, 222-3, 268
gift(s)   4, 10, 21, 51, 112-6, 119, 145, 230
Gilbert   194-5
goal setting   44, 121, 213, 215
goal-to-action conflicts   3, 85-6, 105
goals   2, 4-5, 7-8, 15-17, 29, 38, 46, 48-9, 51, 54, 57, 59, 74, 85-7, 117-8, 123, 148, 162-3, 169-170, 217, 235, 248, 253-4
  powerful   VII, 1, 4, 253-4, 257
  written   5, 7, 16
God   82, 99, 103, 186, 198, 201, 207-8, 216, 221
gods   147, 208
godsend   11
grace   120, 151, 198-202, 224, 233
grades   68, 210
grandfather   - See Father
grandparents   218
Granny   225-6
gratitude   VIII, 103, 211
Greeks   102
ground   IX, 75, 110, 118, 209
grounding   156-7
group(s)   III, VII, 1, 75, 83, 87, 133, 172, 199, 255
Guide(s)   XI, 29, 36, 60, 67, 76, 94, 101, 151-3, 156-7, 173, 199-200, 230, 245
Guru(s)   III, 67, 73-6, 119, 121, 143, 200
gut   39, 117-8, 120, 122, 129

H

habit(s)   11, 13, 27, 29, 164-5, 170, 204, 206
happier   13, 207, 241, 245
happiness   I, II, 12, 37, 47, 62, 133, 177, 191, 211, 216, 248, 252, 254-5
happy   III, 25, 27, 34, 78, 82-3, 111, 186, 208-9, 212, 241
heart   VI, VIII, 63, 81, 120, 147, 156, 190, 214, 240, 242, 264, 273
heaven   72, 82, 101, 205, 208
heights   68, 196, 250
hero   102, 134, 221, 240, 242, 244-5
  super   211, 237-241, 243, 252
hidden decisions
  changing   195, 251-2
  fundamental   64
  inner   193
  resolving   253
  secondary   194

High Self 99-102, 104, 157, 198, 216, 230-3
hospital III, 79-80
hour(s) 32, 159, 230, 251
human body 261
Human Reality 39-40
Huna III, 94-5, 98-9, 103, 216, 231, 267, 271, 274
hurt 68, 76, 118, 165, 216
Hyde, Mr. 189-191
hypnosis 3, 44, 47, 64-5, 121, 176

I

illusion 5, 75, 78
impulse 26, 55-6, 235
inability 75, 126, 194
infant 164, 194-5, 197, 201
information II, 1, 31, 89-90, 115, 120, 144, 151, 159, 177, 230, 257, 274-5
inner beast 190
inner decision, crucial 27
Inner Decision-Maker 93
inner decisions 45, 54, 78, 158, 173
inner knowing 20, 22, 161
instructions II, 4, 29, 104, 217
intent III, XI, 2, 20-2, 26, 41, 61, 65, 75, 100, 104, 111, 123, 180, 198-9, 231-2, 252
  mixed 21-2
intention(s) 1, 20-1, 26, 32, 87, 182, 231-2
interview(s) 39, 131-7, 155, 242, 255, 257-8, 276
intimacy 194, 196
intuition 4, 41, 81, 87-8, 92, 131, 165, 172-3, 216, 229-235, 275

J

Jesus 73, 199-200, 204, 216, 222
Jim 225-6
job III, V, 35, 74, 78, 134-6, 161, 172, 204-5, 242, 245
Judas 239

K

Kahuna(s) 94, 98-101, 103, 106
Kane 188-9
Kid(s) 17, 69, 114, 127-9, 237
knowingness 71, 158
knowledge 2, 4, 7-8, 27, 94-5, 97-9, 101-2, 118, 172, 177, 182, 224, 230
  self- 132, 233
kryptonite 239-240
Ku 99-101, 104-6, 113, 118, 134, 152, 157, 169, 171, 181-3, 188-190, 197, 216, 230-3

L

language 88, 98-9, 103, 122
laugh 16, 69, 123, 239
law(s) V, 26, 39-40, 52, 55-6, 144, 158, 162, 212, 229
layer(s) 164, 246-7, 249-250
legs 81, 99, 165, 209
lesson(s) XI, 29, 70, 110, 113
levels IX, 20, 27-8, 34, 37, 40, 88, 145-6, 165, 168, 198, 217-8, 254, 273
lifetime 4, 164, 231, 253, 275
limp 81, 165
listening 13-4, 26, 105-6, 123, 131, 173, 175, 210
logic 10-1, 13, 25, 36, 39, 44-5, 52, 65-6, 77, 88, 157, 188, 191, 195, 229, 240
  inner 157, 188
  outer 188
Logical Soul® II-X, 1-4, 18, 35-7, 39, 45, 56, 62, 65, 82-3, 88, 93, 95, 103, 106-7, 109, 122, 130-4, 136-7, 139, 143, 147, 151, 155, 158, 161, 163, 165, 168, 171-2, 180, 182, 184, 195-6, 211, 244, 248, 251, 254-5, 257-9, 261, 267, 271
  methodology 35
  process 62, 93, 106, 134, 139, 147, 155, 231, 258
  technique 1, 131, 136, 163, 244, 251
  work 251
logotherapy 207
love I-II, V-VII, XI-XII, 6, 20, 23, 25, 29, 35, 43, 47, 116, 127, 158, 191, 194, 196-200, 204, 211, 234, 242, 268, 273, 275
lovers 242
Low Self 99-102, 104, 106, 152, 169, 188, 230
lynchpin decision, hidden 243

M

Madonna 242-4
magic 5-6, 8, 11, 16-7, 31, 33, 39, 98, 102
Maharishi 36, 74-5, 161, 266
mana 100, 157, 232
manifest(s) 9, 17-9, 21, 27, 36-40, 55-7, 102, 146, 188, 214, 231, 238
manifestation 11, 18, 19, 21, 39-40, 55-6, 232
  normal cycle of 19
  error cycle of 21
Maslow 33-7, 197, 237, 273
master(s) XI, 22-3, 60, 75, 119, 134, 170, 199-200
mastermind 83, 172
masterpiece 190
material(s) II, 11, 97, 103, 255

matter(s)   45-6, 128, 169, 180, 193, 197, 203, 205, 208, 210, 243, 269, 272
Max Freedom Long   85, 94, 98, 103, 230, 274
meditation   1, 36-8, 44, 72-5, 86, 225, 273
meme(s)   208-9, 211, 234-5, 240, 249, 274-5
memory   4, 41, 49, 55, 63-4, 72, 87-8, 100-1, 104-6, 114, 126, 165, 169, 213-4, 230-1, 233, 235, 274
   ancient   234-5
   body   64
   cellular   213-4
mental pollution   9-12
mentor(s)   1, 121, 166, 168, 172-3, 207, 255
Michael   I-III, V, VII, IX-XI, 91, 109-116, 187, 226, 256, 267
Middle Self   99-105, 230
mind viruses   2, 121, 233-4
minutes   I-II, V, VII, 1-2, 15-6, 18, 39, 49, 57, 79, 81, 88, 114, 116, 121-2, 130, 132, 139, 147, 151, 153, 155, 159, 161, 251, 254
miracles   40, 94, 98, 184
money   III, XII, 7-8, 10, 27, 29, 31, 35, 44, 54, 59, 74, 92-3, 112-5, 125, 127, 134-5, 137, 145-6, 150, 167-170, 173, 180, 185, 194-5, 247, 249-250
  accepting   10, 115, 168
  amount of   145, 167-8
  earning   170, 249-250
  making   59, 167-8
mother   III, 28, 39, 81, 114, 194-5, 201, 217, 225, 242
  grand   35, 222
  great-grand   70
motivation   3, 5-6, 9, 11, 26-9, 33-5, 38-9, 44, 52, 97, 118, 120, 132, 143, 151, 162, 165, 218, 259, 273
multiple hidden decisions, changing   251
muscle   3, 52-3, 60-1, 89-90, 100, 110-1, 113, 129, 131-2, 137, 139-140, 142-5, 157, 163, 168, 181, 194, 218, 235, 258-9, 262, 272
muscle testing   52-3, 60-1, 89-90, 100, 110-1, 129, 131-2, 137, 139, 142-5, 157, 168, 181, 194, 218, 235, 258-9

N

nature   37, 190, 206, 208, 212, 217
navigate   18, 20, 235
needles   79-81
negative thought(s)   7, 11-12, 30, 121, 162
negativity   12, 15
nerve facilitation   164, 170
nerve tissue   164
nervous system   35-6, 46, 63, 87, 126, 155, 164-5, 169, 195, 232
non-changeable hidden decisions   193

O

obsessive-compulsive disorder (OCD)   198
OCD (obsessive-compulsive disorder)   198
onion   248-9, 251-2, 254
operations   3, 264
Oprah Winfrey   XI, 20-1
organic-decision-bound   197-8, 200
organic decisions   122, 195, 197-8
  unchanging   197
outcome(s)   19, 26, 41, 45-7, 54, 56, 106, 188

P

pain   17, 43, 62, 78-9, 81, 122, 124, 188, 197, 222, 231, 251
painful   43, 184
paradigm   97, 148-150, 176, 195, 251
paradox   9, 187, 275
parents   VII, 17, 68, 73, 125, 195, 197, 209, 217-8, 222, 271-2, 275
  grand   218
partner   53, 90, 92, 132, 135, 140, 142, 158, 199
path   VI, 28, 37, 71, 106, 156, 168, 172-3, 178, 200, 226, 263, 273
pathways   170
patients   33, 36, 52-3, 82, 93, 125-6, 175-6, 180, 182-3, 255
peace   XII, 71, 142, 144, 217, 219, 224-5
peel(ing)   187, 248-9, 251-2, 254
persistence   16-18
Personal Archetypes   152, 181
personal power   95, 171
personal story   149-150, 237-8, 244-5, 251-2
PGP (Powerful Goals Program)   VII, 1
phase(s)   131-2, 135-6, 145, 147, 150, 155, 157, 159, 206
phobias   183-4, 196
physiology   120, 122, 128-9, 165, 225
pollution   9-12, 273
polygraph   142-4, 259, 262-4
positive thinking   11-12, 30, 78, 148, 273
power   IX, XI-XII, 2, 4, 8-9, 15, 18, 20-2, 29-30, 38, 41, 45, 52, 61-3, 65, 70-1, 82, 93-5, 98-9, 103-4, 106, 109, 141, 158, 171, 173, 188, 190, 199, 203, 207, 209, 221-4, 238, 243, 248, 252, 254, 260, 274, 276
  raw   21-2, 63
  super   70-1, 238
powerful   VI-VII, X, 1, 4, 7-8, 18, 20, 89, 92, 98, 100, 105, 111, 118, 140, 151, 156-8, 163, 166, 169, 194, 199, 207, 213, 217, 239, 253-4, 257, 274
powerful affirmations, most   111
Powerful Goals Program^{tm} - See PGP
practitioner   54, 60, 64, 75, 80, 92
pray   101, 104, 230-2
prayer   100-102, 231

problem(s)   V, 2, 9-10, 27-8, 34, 39, 46, 54, 60, 62, 68, 75, 80, 86, 93, 118, 125, 130, 149, 176-7, 184, 198, 210, 249, 259, 261, 266
procrastination   170-1
program(s)   III, VII, 1, 7-9, 45, 47-8, 113, 115, 120, 162-3, 166, 168, 180, 184, 199, 231, 252, 261-2, 272
programming   9, 64, 115, 134, 158, 165, 188, 251
project(s)   83, 128, 144, 173, 222, 275
psychologist   II, VI, IX, XI, 33, 45, 176
psychology   33-4, 99, 102, 175, 185
pyramid   34-5

Q
questions   61, 127-8, 132, 134-7, 141-2, 150, 181, 195

R
reality   3, 5, 7-8, 11, 17, 34, 39-40, 47, 118, 136, 149, 157, 177, 187, 195, 201, 206, 208, 213
  law of human   39-40
  Santa Claus Theory of   17
Realization(s)   51, 71-2, 210
recovery   38
redundancy   164
release(d)   XI, 72, 121, 151, 180, 182-3, 224-6, 248-9, 266
relief   VI, 37, 39, 80-1, 83, 128, 182, 200
resistance   15, 37, 41, 168, 171, 173, 175, 179-180
resolution   14, 37, 45-6, 80, 131, 147, 155, 157, 257, 262-3
resources   10-11, 39, 103, 161-2
responsibility   II, V, 40, 48, 215
resting brains   36
resurrection   216
reward   16, 20, 142
rickets   80-81
ritual(s)   60, 202-9, 211, 215
Robbins, Anthony (Tony)   6, 20-1, 94, 98, 167
root(s)   2, 12, 29, 35, 82, 99, 119, 121-2, 149, 203, 215-6, 248

S
sadness   26, 223, 231
saint   200, 221, 242, 244
Schwartz, Dr. David   6, 8, 20, 31
script(s)   242-3, 245, 251-2
secret(s)   V, 3, 8, 27, 31, 33, 54, 70, 73, 94, 97-99, 104, 107, 151, 176, 223, 238-9, 241, 247, 274
secret identity   73, 238-9, 241
Seed of Failure, see SOF
Seed of Success, see SOS
seeds   29, 86, 97, 118-9, 191

self-actualization   34, 273
self-deception   12, 243, 249
self-sabotage   I-III, 2-5, 9-10, 21, 35, 52, 188, 210, 248, 255
selves   94, 97, 98-100, 102-4, 188, 230
  three   94, 97, 99-100, 102-3, 230
session(s)   VI, VIII, XI, 36-7, 39, 81, 83, 116, 125, 130, 132-3, 137, 142, 144, 158, 163-5, 168, 175, 195
shoulder   29, 110-1, 205
sign(s)   90-1, 103, 217
signal(s)   124, 164, 232
skill(s)   131-2, 170, 176, 196, 253
sleep   7, 36, 66, 75, 77, 119, 164, 210, 223
SOF (Seed of Failure)   26, 97, 118-121, 125-6, 129, 151, 161-2, 161, 170
SOF Syndrome   162, 168
solution   27, 30, 44, 143, 197
Soma   - See Brigitte
SOS (Seed of Success)   119-120, 151, 161, 256
soul   II-III, V-VIII, X, 1-6, 10, 13, 18, 20, 35-7, 39, 45, 52, 56, 62, 65-6, 77, 82-3, 88, 93, 95, 103, 106-7, 109, 117, 122, 130-4, 136-7, 139, 143, 147, 151, 155, 158, 161, 163, 165, 168, 171-2, 180, 182, 184, 195-6, 210-211, 231, 244, 248, 251-2, 254-9, 261, 267-8, 270
source   II, 4, 22, 35, 37, 46, 51, 61, 92, 106, 122, 124, 221, 232, 234
speaker(s)   VI, 6-7, 11
spirit   IX, 17, 82, 95, 99-101, 104, 208, 216-7, 224, 230
spiritual   X, 20, 60, 80, 200, 203, 208, 227, 233, 238, 249, 254
split   9, 32, 35-8
split mind   32, 35, 38
stability   62, 151
stars   22-3, 71, 210
statement(s)   20, 53-4, 61, 88-9, 91-3, 111-3, 116, 126, 129-130, 136-7, 139-140, 142, 145-6, 150-1, 155, 169, 171-2, 180, 217
  negative   91, 137
  positive   91, 111, 129
stimulus/stimuli   63, 80, 122
story/stories   V, 4, 22, 29, 80, 97-8, 103, 114-5, 120, 129, 141, 149-150, 152, 176, 178-9, 181, 199, 223, 235, 237-245, 248, 251-2
strength   2, 18, 30, 43, 47, 110, 140, 144, 161-2, 177, 180, 209, 233, 245
stress   34, 73-4, 126, 142, 144, 183, 251
struggle   III, 17-18, 37, 41, 77, 198
stuff   4, 10, 28, 40, 64, 76, 83, 88, 120, 123, 128, 133, 164, 183, 196, 211, 213-4
subconscious mind   3, 13, 27, 35, 37, 53, 64, 85, 98, 164, 169, 176, 183, 213, 258
subject   36, 64, 79, 98, 100, 103, 143, 164, 202

The Logical Soul®

success   I-II, V, X, 4, 6-10, 15-6, 20, 22-3, 25-31, 38, 41, 43-5, 47, 60, 65, 74, 86, 97, 117-9, 125, 133, 147, 151, 158, 161-2, 168, 170-1, 173, 190-1, 194, 205, 219, 242, 249, 254, 256
successful   V, 32, 38, 48, 60, 118, 134, 170, 172, 232, 250
super hero   - See hero, super
super villain   238-9, 241
Superman   68, 70, 239
survival   8, 10, 45, 149, 195-6, 205, 207-8, 259
survival decisions   10
   pre-verbal   45
symptoms   34, 37, 61, 74, 80, 127, 189

T

taboo(s)   203-6, 208, 211
tap(ping)   4, 29, 44, 56-7, 60, 62, 64-5, 105, 205, 248
tape(s)   6-7, 47-8, 165
Taylor, Dr. Jill   37
teach   28-31, 49, 74, 76, 90, 98, 135, 199-200
teacher(s)   VIII, 3, 11, 68, 70, 73-4, 168, 208-9, 273
technique(s)   II-III, V, VII, 1-3, 27-8, 36, 49, 52-4, 56, 62, 65, 82, 88, 92, 111, 115, 131, 136, 143-4, 147, 158, 163, 209, 244, 247-8, 250-1, 257-8, 268, 270, 273
teeth   39, 204, 206
telescope   71-2
temple(s)   200-2
test(ing)   3, 38, 52-4, 60-2, 65, 79, 87-93, 100, 110-112, 115, 129, 131-2, 136-7, 139-145, 150, 157, 163, 168-9, 171, 173, 180-1, 194, 218, 225, 235, 249, 257-262, 265, 271-2
therapist(s)   VIII, 38, 53, 143, 175-7, 182-4
therapy   III, 28, 158, 165, 180, 182-3, 207
thinking big   6-7, 31
three selves   94, 97, 99-103, 230
threshold   156, 164, 260
TM (Transcendental Meditation^{TM})   36, 73, 273-4
tool(s)   X-XI, 27, 42, 82, 90, 105, 129, 142-4, 149, 182, 207, 215, 252-3, 254, 259
tradition   75, 144, 213, 216, 221
Transcendental Meditation^{TM} *see* TM
transformation   38, 61-2, 6, 158, 163, 184, 195, 248
trauma   193, 195-6, 224
True Grace   200-201
trust   VI, VIII, 80, 92, 101, 140-1, 143, 151-3, 177, 181, 244, 253
truth   30, 97, 137, 141, 144-5, 149-150, 158, 217, 238, 240
TV   V-VI, 10, 68, 75, 187-8, 204, 275
Type(s)   9, 41, 59-60, 6, 122, 207, 270

U

Uhane   99, 101, 106, 157, 169, 230, 233, 260-262
Unihipili   99, 157, 230
victim(s)   37, 40, 75, 83, 189
villain   238-9, 241-2
virus(es)   2, 121, 233-4, 274-5
vision(s)   29, 70, 72
voice   11, 13-14, 144, 148, 173
voice changes   144
voice stress analysis – See CVSA

W

Wall, the   61-2, 135, 147-8, 151, 175-182, 184
wealth   I-II, IX, 7, 20-1, 31, 46-7, 183, 191
website   III, VII, XII, 92, 132, 163, 223
whale   13, 104-6
wholeness   XII, 36, 38, 48
wife   III, 1, 7, 55, 77-9, 82, 109, 213-4, 223, 226, 242
willpower   17-18, 33, 52
wisdom   29, 31, 44, 51-2, 65, 98, 121, 187, 218
wizard   242-4
work   IV, VI, VIII, IX-XI, 1, 8, 15-18, 20, 34-5, 39-40, 45, 47-8, 51-2, 55, 62, 65-6, 74, 78, 82-3, 87, 92-4, 102, 109, 112, 114, 122-3, 125, 130, 132-3, 140-2, 147, 161, 168-170, 172, 175-6, 179-180, 182, 196, 199, 205-6, 214, 222-3, 239, 249-251, 254-5, 257-8, 274
workshop(s)   VII, 54, 132, 255
world   8, 13-16, 18, 20, 22, 27, 29, 39-40, 45, 47, 55, 67-70, 74-5, 103, 118, 125, 143, 149, 151, 158, 170, 178-9, 186, 197, 200, 204, 215-7, 221, 231-2, 234, 239, 243-4, 250-1, 255
  cartoon   68-70
  new   14, 70, 221, 251
worldview   45, 148-9, 211
writer(s)   VII-VIII, 6, 82, 136-7, 190, 250

www.ingramcontent.com/pod-product-compliance
Lightning Source LLC
Chambersburg PA
CBHW071659170426
43195CB00039B/2241